S0-BKF-266

EQUIPPING THE SAINTS

A Guide for Giving to Faith-Based Organizations

EQUIPPING THE SAINTS

A GUIDE FOR GIVING TO FAITH-BASED

ORGANIZATIONS

BARBARA J. ELLIOTT

TEMPLETON FOUNDATION PRESS

Philadelphia and London

Templeton Foundation Press

300 Conshohocken State Road, Suite 550

West Conshohocken, PA 19428

www.templetonpress.org

© 2005 by Barbara J. Elliott

Produced in cooperation with the Foundation for American Renewal,

Indianapolis, Indiana.

All rights reserved. No part of this book may be used or reproduced, stored in a retrieval

system, or transmitted in any form or by any means, electronic, mechanical, photocopying,

recording, or otherwise, without the written permission of Templeton Foundation Press.

Templeton Foundation Press helps intellectual leaders and others learn about science

research on aspects of realities, invisible and intangible. Spiritual realities include unlimited

love, accelerating creativity, worship, and the benefits of purpose in persons

and in the cosmos.

Designed and typeset by Kachergis Book Design

Library of Congress Cataloging-in-Publication Data

Elliott, Barbara J.

Equipping the saints : a guide for giving to faith-based organizations

/ Barbara J. Elliott.

p. cm.

ISBN 1-932031-88-x (pbk. : alk. paper)   1. Church charities—United

States.   2. Endowments—United States.   3. Church charities—United

States—Evaluation.   I. Title.

HV530.E55 2004

361.7'5—dc22

2004016100

Printed in the United States of America

05   06   07   08   10   9   8   7   6   5   4   3   2   1

Contents

Introduction, by William A. Schambra — 7

1. **Why Give to Faith-Based Organizations?** — 11
   Agents of Social Change, 11
   The Spectrum of Faith-Based Organizations, 13
   From "Faith Founded" to "Faith Saturated," 14

2. **Due Diligence** — 16
   Beyond the Culture Clash, 16
   Questions to Ask Before You Give, 17
   Gift Size and Analysis Should be Commensurate, 18

3. **Evaluating Programs** — 21
   Drucker's Self-Assessment Tool, 21
   The "Faith Factor," 22
   Documented Results, 23
   Outcomes-Based Evaluation, 25

4. **What to Look For: Signs of Health** — 28
   Signs of Health in Faith-Based Groups, 29
   Penetrating Questions to Ask, 30
   Peer-to-Peer Advice: Tom McCallie, 32
   Beware of Red Flags, 32

5. **Capacity Building: Leveraging Impact** — 34
   What Foundations Can Learn from Venture Capitalists, 35
   Curriculum for Capacity Building, 36
   Examples of Donor Engagement:
       Leveraging Promise: The Maclellan Foundation, 38
       Social Capital plus Competence: Fred Smith, 39
       Entrepreneurial Skills: David Weekley, 40
       Building Capacity Across the Country: Pew, 40
       Generating Revenue: Social Entrepreneurs, 41

6. **Ways to Give: Models in Action**   44

The Gathering, 44

Philanthropy Roundtable, 44

Generous Giving, 45

Community Foundations, 46

Christian Community Foundations, 47

Jewish Philanthropy, 48

Kingdom Oil: Jay Bennett, 48

Taking Personal Initiative: Foster Friess, 49

Little League and Hope Academy: Bob Muzikowski, 50

Creating a Nonprofit Campus, 51

Intersection with Business: David Oelfke, 51

Entrepreneurial Brainstorming: Paul McDonald, 52

Nehemiah Strategy: A City-Wide Vision, 52

Strengths of Intermediaries, 53

Suggestions from the Field, 54

Conclusion: Motivation Matters   57

Moses Maimonides on *Tzedakah*, 57

The Motive of *Agape*, 59

An Investment in the Eternal, 60

Notes, 61

**Appendix. Donor's Toolbox for Evaluationg Faith-Based Organizations
    by The Legacy Group, Inc.**   63

Tool 1. Donor's Giving Interest Inventory:
    John L. Stanley, 63

Tool 2. The Giving Continuum: Defining Your Approach
    to Giving, 66

Tool 3. What to Look for in a Philanthropic Advisor:
    Peter A. Giersch, 67

Tool 4. Tax and Legal Ramifications of Giving to Faith-Based
    Organizations: Patricia G. Woehrer, 69

Tool 5. Analyzing Nonprofit Financial Statements:
    Mary Kay Mark, 73

Tool 6. Faith-Based Organizations from A to Z: A Donor's Guide:
    Barbara J. Elliott, 76

Tool 7. Checklist for a Site Visit: Mary Kay Mark, 78

Tool 8. Checklist for Due Diligence: Patricia G. Woehrer, 80

Contact Information, 85

Introduction

The most inspiring and rewarding part of my job as a program officer for ten years at the Lynde and Harry Bradley Foundation was the all-too-infrequent site visit to one of our faith-based grantees in Milwaukee's inner city. Since I was otherwise confined to a comfortable office, plowing through grant proposals or puzzling over project budgets, it was all too easy to forget why I was there and who was really helped by my work. But such questions were quickly laid to rest with a visit to the late Bill Lock's Community Enterprises of Greater Milwaukee, or Cordelia Taylor's Family House, or Ramon Candeleria's Latino Community Center.

Here, I witnessed saints at work. Their lives had been touched and transformed by faith, and now they were kindling the same transformation in the lives of others. Whether they were preparing former welfare recipients for gainful employment, or easing the final hours of an elderly homeless person, or pulling young people out of gangs, they pursued their work with the quiet but unshakable confidence that they were answering thereby a summons from God. The message to their hard-pressed communities: just as we have been carried by faith through the most trying times and most demanding challenges, so shall your burdens be made lighter by faith. No one—certainly not this otherwise complacent program officer—could witness the work of such profound faith under such trying circumstances without going away re-inspirited and renewed. Thus was I reminded of the work I was about as a program officer: helping my foundation to equip the saints.

Given the Bradley Foundation's willing support of faith-based groups—it has made grants ranging from a few thousand dollars for a new roof at a storefront ministry to a $1 million grant to Pastor Sedgwick Daniel's Holy Redeemer Church of God in Christ for a community center—it has always been somewhat puzzling to me that other foundations and donors seemed so hesitant about supporting such groups. It is particularly perplexing at a time when, as Barbara Elliott notes herein, social science research has begun to document the effectiveness of faith-based organizations at solving social problems, and when major public figures of all political stripes, including the President of the United States, have argued that even government should be prepared to assist faith-based institutions within the limits prescribed by the U.S. Constitution. But there are plausible reasons for this hesitancy.

Peering out from foundation or corporate offices toward low-income inner-city or rural communities, it is often very difficult to see beyond a handful of large, nationally known nonprofits, lavishly equipped with aggressive publicity and fund-raising arms. These organizations are typically secular, or religious only in a rather nominal way. The faith-based groups discussed in this volume, by contrast, are almost invisible from privileged enclaves downtown or in the suburbs. They are located in old storefronts in the toughest neighborhoods, with mismatched furniture, water-stained ceilings, and duct tape on the carpet. They are often manned by unpaid volunteers, whose chief credential for service is that they themselves have, by the grace of God, transcended the circumstances out of which they are now trying to lift others. It's usually more efficient for them to scrape by on small donations from their friends or from their own pockets than to try to master the demanding art of fund-raising and report writing. And yet these are the groups that are, person by person and block by block, reclaiming individuals and neighborhoods otherwise forgotten by the major institutions of government and philanthropy.

How do we equip these saints? How do we bridge the chasm between donor and grassroots, faith-based group? We need a guide—someone who is comfortable in both worlds, and who can mark the paths back and forth between them. Thankfully, we have such a guide in Barbara Elliott. Mrs. Elliott is a compelling speaker and widely published author of books and articles on the role of faith in civic renewal. She has worked for major national think tanks and publications and in the White House, and has received awards at the hand of the President of the United States. She is at home in the most powerful and wealthy circles in the nation.

And yet, as this volume will demonstrate, she is not content to remain in that world. Her primary passion is to seek out and bring to our attention precisely those smaller, faith-based, grassroots efforts that are otherwise so easily overlooked. She moves with ease in that world as well, because she, too, values the deep spiritual nourishment and enrichment that she finds there.

This volume, then, is a guide for donors who, perhaps intrigued by all the talk about faith-based initiatives, may have pondered helping them but were uncertain of the best path into that world. Mrs. Elliott and her colleagues at The Legacy Group, Inc., provide the sorts of observations, suggestions, precautions, and checklists that any donor would need to make prudent, effective grants to smaller organizations. But they are offered without the patronizing air of superiority that typically accompanies such devices. That is because they understand that the leaders of successful grassroots groups—and national spokesmen for them like Robert Woodson at the National Center for Neighborhood Enterprise—are the primary authorities on the sources of and solutions to America's social ills.

Consequently, this volume will show the donor where it is useful to turn off the well-paved highway leading to the coffers of the massive, bureaucratic, impersonal, and therefore often less effective social service agencies. This is no mean accomplishment in a philanthropic world where the customary approach is for initiatives to be cooked up by academically credentialed experts back at foundation headquarters, which will then be enthusiastically embraced by the "usual suspects"—the large nonprofits with well-paid professional grant writers, who can only profess astonishment at the degree of congruence between their nonprofit's fervent wish and the foundation's serene command.

Following the paths marked out by Barbara Elliott in this volume, prospective donors will soon find that they, too, are able to move freely between the worlds of philanthropy and faith-based, grassroots initiatives. They will then come upon their own Bill Locks, Cordelia Taylors, and Ramon Candelerias, who will serve as local guides through the rich, diverse landscapes of the neighborhoods they love and serve. These local guides will be able to offer new sources of wisdom and guidance, rooted in local knowledge, practical experience, and a keen understanding of which local leaders are religious charlatans and which are individuals of genuine spiritual integrity. I know that Mrs. Elliott agrees that this is the sort of donors' understanding that can never be captured in one guidebook. But her guidebook is the indispensable first step toward the acquisition of that larger, more subtle, more intuitive, and finally, more profound understanding.

Donors following Mrs. Elliott's guidance into that world will soon find that they, too, have discovered previously unimagined sources of spiritual nourishment and refreshment, in the least likely of places. Especially in moments of doubt about the value of their work and gifts, they, too, will find reasons to make site visits to favorite grantees, allegedly to check up on the stewardship of resources, but in fact simply to listen to words of calm assurance about the work of the Spirit in the world, to witness firsthand previously forsaken souls now walking the earth free of addictions, poverty, and despair, and to be in the presence of people who unmistakably bear the marks of the hand of God.

We begin this journey with a desire to equip the saints. But the journey leads us to a place where the saints equip us.

William A. Schambra
Director, Bradley Center for Philanthropy and Civic Renewal
Hudson Institute

one

Why Give to Faith-Based Organizations?

Faith-based organizations are producing civic value in the lives that they are transforming. Sociological research is beginning to document the social change these groups accomplish, and civic-minded donors are investing in the groups that are successful. As one foundation executive put it at a conference of donors recently, "We don't care what faith the organization has as long as it's producing results. We're investing in faith as an agent of change."

A large and growing body of literature documents the "faith factor" in helping addicts leave drugs, reducing recidivism in prisoners, diminishing criminal behavior in adolescents, preventing teen pregnancy, and renewing blighted communities. Whether providing international emergency services, inner-city fatherhood initiatives, or job training, faith-based groups are intervening to make lives whole. While much remains to be done in serious analysis of their outcomes, the preliminary evidence indicates that faith is a potent source of human change that can offer a significant return on investment.

 "We don't care what faith the organization has as long as it's producing results. We're investing in faith as an agent of change."

Small, grassroots organizations rooted in the neighborhoods their leaders serve are often the most effective. Many of these groups toil in relative obscurity, not even a blip on the radar screen of most foundations, and almost invisible to individual donors. Yet people like Robert Woodson of the National Center for Neighborhood Enterprise who have systematically sought them out can validate their significant effect in renewal at the grassroots level. They are penetrating the root causes of human misery.

Peter Drucker, the renowned management expert, claims that the measure of any nonprofit's success is expressed in changed human lives. Faith-based organizations (FBOs) specialize in changing human lives, and their work's civic value surpasses the monetary value of their services. Every drug addict who returns to sobriety and employment, every prisoner who abandons a life of crime, every at-risk youngster who finds stability, testifies to these groups' bottom line of human and civic value. To the extent that faith-based groups produce reliable employees and taxpayers, thereby reducing the burden on public support, they contribute to their fellow citizens' quality of life.

 Faith-based organizations are penetrating the root causes of human misery.

In the coming intergenerational transfer of wealth, $41.3 trillion will change hands. An estimated $5–10 trillion will pour into the philanthropic sector over the next three to ten years. Financial and legal advisors typically counsel effectively on setting up a vehicle to preserve wealth or avoid taxes but lack expertise in guiding prudent giving. Because faith-based organizations serve as potent engines of social change, donors should seriously consider them. Many faith-based organizations are producing tangible results in transforming lives. However, not all of them are equally effective. Responsible consideration of faith-based organizations must include a dispassionate analysis of their strengths and weaknesses. To assist in the process, there are philanthropic advisors who specialize in this sector, but they are scarce.

This guide is intended to assist potential donors in navigating the waters of the faith-based universe. Every donor has individual interests, inclinations, and intentions. Giving is intensely personal, and if it is aligned with one's own deepest convictions, it can bring joy. Different faith traditions have different emphases, and the spectrum across providers corresponds to the diversity across donors. Theology and methodology differ and individual groups address very different populations and needs. Composing a personal mission statement for giving can effectively narrow the universe of possibilities to a manageable pool to consider. (A donor's giving interest inventory is included at the end of this book to facilitate the process.)

 Giving is intensely personal, and if it is aligned with one's own deepest convictions, it can bring joy.

A reservoir of good will animates the country for religious causes. More than 87 percent of all the giving in the United States comes from households that contribute to religious congregations. These donors also support secular causes and, in fact, give three times more than those who support only secular organizations. "The extraordinary generosity of religious givers knows very few boundaries," says former Independent Sector President and CEO Sara E. Melendez.[1]

In looking at faith-based organizations, several clusters of issues require thought. A donor should consider how effectively faith-based organizations go beyond good intentions to produce outcomes. Ascertain whether they are run as sustainable nonprofits, with sound management and clean financials. Then consider the kind of involvement, which may include giving not only money or materials but also time or professional skills. A group of donors acting together or a community foundation may provide a vehicle for combined giving, for those who prefer not to go it alone. Consider what you seek for yourself in the process: perhaps social return on investment, implementation of a strategy, or spiritual reward.

This guide addresses each of these clusters of issues, drawing on the experience of donors who have supported faith-based organizations. Seasoned advisors offer helpful tools for the process in the appendices. They address these essential questions:

1. Am I interested in what this organization does? Does it fit with my convictions, beliefs, and interests?
2. Does this work change human lives for the better? Can I verify outcomes?
3. Is the organization run well as a sustainable nonprofit?
4. What do I want to give—time, talent, money, or some combination? How do I want to give?

The Spectrum of Faith-Based Organizations

What is the scope of faith-based giving in America? Of $240.9 billion given to private philanthropy funds in 2002, nearly $84.3 billion was directed toward religious organizations.[2] They use the money not only for houses of worship and teaching of the faithful, but dedicate a significant portion of it to serving their neighbors. Sociologist Ram Cnaan documents that about 90 percent of America's 350,000 congregations (all faiths combined) serve their communities through at least one program, most often aiding impoverished neighborhood families who are not members of their own congregation.[3] This number excludes the separate nonprofits established by people of faith, with or without a direct congregational affiliation, who also care for the needy. The annual value of faith-based organizations' contributions to social welfare in the United States is estimated at $36 billion.[4] They serve an estimated 70 million Americans annually.[5]

The spectrum of faith-based organizations spans a wide continuum, differentiated by motivation, intention, degree of religiosity, and results. They are different sizes and shapes and their legal arrangements differ. While most of the nation's 350,000 congregations offer programs as a part of their community outreach, an increasing number of congregations are establishing separate nonprofit corporations with a 501(c)(3) tax-exempt status to do faith-based work in the community. And other faith-based organizations, the so-called "para-church" organizations, operate fully independently of any religious congregation. Community Development Corporations (CDCs) are also springing up, particularly among African American churches.

 Faith-based organizations serve 70 million Americans annually with services valued at $36 billion.

Faith-based organizations vary in intention and intensity, ranging from faith-neutral to faith-saturated. A donor will most likely want to find a fit that reflects his or her own theology and intentionality. Clear differences mark denominational tendencies and traditions.

Faith Founded

At one end are organizations founded by people because of their religious convictions, but which provide services of an essentially secular nature. Faith provided the initial motivation, but it is not actively manifested in the programs. There are probably thousands of these.

Faith Unspoken

Next on the continuum are the programs founded because of faith, whose mission states their religious motivation, but whose programs are executed without teaching or preaching. For example, congregations may provide a food pantry or clothes closet for recipients who know that the staff and volunteers come from local houses of worship, but the interaction is an *unspoken* embodiment of their convictions. Church-based mentors in public schools demonstrate this approach, for example.

Faith Optional

These programs may have religious symbols as a part of the facility where the services or programs take place, creating a space where faith is acknowledged. A crucifix might grace the wall, books of scripture may lie open. The blessing before meals may reference God, although participation is not required. Doctors or nurses in a clinic may offer to pray with patients if they wish, although prayer is never forced on anyone. If asked, staff or volunteers, who are people of faith, may share the source of their belief.

Faith Integrated

The next kind of program offers some explicitly religious teaching woven together with other nonreligious elements. In addition to job skills training, resume-writing instruction, and parenting classes, a Bible study class on character may be offered to women leaving welfare. Or, a parochial school could require morning chapel attendance, before teaching the scriptural basis of literature or the role of the church in history. The faith element plays an integral role in the organization's overall approach.

Faith Explicit

This kind of work promulgates faith through its programs, publications, and relationships in order to change behavior. It might be a prison program that intends to change the motivation of prisoners through faith in order to reduce recidivism. Faith-explicit organizations include those that advocate abstinence for teens because of faith, for example, or provide Christian fatherhood programs based on biblical teaching. They seek to change convictions through the agent of faith, which can result in changed human behavior.

Faith Saturated

These programs are not only motivated by faith, but use faith as their method. Some drug rehabilitation programs and homeless shelters practice this approach, which consists of a total immersion in religious teaching, worship, and scripture study. Staff members and volunteers, all people of faith, mentor the participants through example as well as through words. In faith-saturated programs, the religious component cannot be sorted out from the others, as the whole approach is an integrated manifestation of the experience of faith. The explicit goal seeks to transform people over a sustained period of time in a way that touches the wellspring of their motivation.

Some donors will undoubtedly find several of these approaches anathema, measured against their own convictions and comfort levels. Remember, however, that people who go to these institutions for services can freely go elsewhere if they are uncomfortable with what they find there. The same holds true for donors, who are free to find the approach that resonates with their own faith and intentionality.

Donors should be aware that many faith-based organizations move up and down on this continuum and may not fit neatly into one category. Some churches that offer welfare-to-work programs have isolated the secular services they provide from those that have an explicit faith content, creating another legal entity for the portion of their work that receives government or other secular funding. Some faith-based organizations have experienced "mission creep," losing their faith orientation in the pursuit of secular funding, whether public or private. Some organizations change their character over time, like any number of universities in the United States that were founded by religious congregations but have abandoned religious content. Digging deeper will reveal an organization's true motivation and current status.

two

Due Diligence

Andrew Carnegie remarked that it is at least as hard to give money away intelligently as it is to make it in the first place. Some people insist this task is even harder. Making donations with a real understanding of what an organization does and how well it works requires diligence. A donor should assess the organizational viability of the nonprofit. Even though faith-based organizations are largely program-driven to serve human needs, they still must be intelligently run as nonprofits to guarantee organizational stability. A particular soft spot in many faith-based organizations is management. Sometimes, charismatic leaders with huge hearts and big visions lack the managerial talents required to run organizations smoothly, raise money, and pay the bills on time. As such an organization grows, it may reach a critical point when the leader realizes his or her or limitations and finds a staff person to accept these tasks, or the organization stops developing.

 A soft spot in many faith-based organizations is management. And they are chronically understaffed.

Beyond the Culture Clash

Some leaders think that because they are doing ministry professional standards are unnecessary, even "unspiritual." Many faith-based organizations are chronically understaffed, compounding even conscientious managers' difficulties in running the office. Some board directors do not see the need for a staff or even a salary for the leader of a faith-based organization. Other leaders do not fund-raise because they believe, as a matter of faith, that they will simply be given whatever they need. These cultures clash when foundation directors want to see a plan.

Jana Mullins of the Rockwell Fund in Houston talked to one of the foundation's applicants who had been running a ministry for thirty years and asked the elderly woman if she had a plan for succession. "The Lord will provide," the woman smiled.

"Yes, yes," nodded Mullins, "but don't you have an earthly plan?" Precisely this kind of conversation can unnerve some donors. It is more comforting to encounter people who pray as if everything depends on God, but work as if everything depends on them. The directness with which some leaders speak about their faith can be jarring. It is not unusual for a leader to say, "The Lord told me to . . ." and roll out an edict with conviction. The Lord does indeed speak, but it is also true that not everyone who says "Lord, Lord" has necessarily received a word from him. Discernment is a spiritual gift, and a wise donor needs it.

> "The Lord will provide," the woman smiled.
> "Yes, yes, but don't you have an earthly plan?"

Faith-based organizations tend to run on a wing and a prayer, with an operation held together with duct tape. A passion to serve drives the people who go into this kind of work. Few of them have any nonprofit management training or business experience, which means they are learning on the job. For that reason, it is wise to take a good look at their operations. Terry Bell of the Rockwell Fund cautions, "Faith-based groups can be short-sighted and inefficient, just like any other organization." Carolyn Watson adds, "But they sometimes have the hubris on top of it because they say, 'We're doing the Lord's work.'" Both report that they have made many grants to faith-based organizations that have proven successful. But they advocate common sense and caution, just as one would exercise in making any grant.

Questions to Ask Before You Give

Larry Lloyd is the founder of Hope Christian Community Foundation in Memphis, Tennessee, who has since become a college president. Earlier in his career, as the president of the Memphis Leadership Foundation, he started and nurtured to maturity more than twenty ministries and faith-centered community initiatives. After moving to the philanthropic sector, he was instrumental in advising donors who have invested significantly in faith-based organizations. As Lloyd worked with donors in navigating these waters, he brought the experience from both sides of the giving equation to bear in a way that few people can. He recommends that donors ask the following questions before they give to a faith-based organization.

- Does the organization have a clear mission statement?
- Does it have three to four strategic objectives and specific goals for the year?
- What is considered success? Can the organization state results?
- Does it have a board of directors, male and female, beyond family members, that is representative of the community served?
- Are accounting practices sound?

- What is the proportion of administrative overhead? If it is more than 15 percent for local groups and more than 25 percent for national, that's a red flag.
- Does the organization have valid 501(c)(3) status and a filed 990 form?
- Does it get a financial audit? If not, why not?
- Does it have a statement of values and faith?
- What are the credentials of the staff?
- What does a site visit reveal about them?

Gift Size and Analysis Should be Commensurate

The depth of analysis should probably parallel the size of the gift. With a gift of $5,000 or less, it would probably suffice to look at an organization's proposal and publications, check for valid documentation of its tax-exempt status, and inquire about its reputation in the community, perhaps getting a second opinion from another funder. Larger amounts merit more investigation.

For donations of more than $10,000, a donor will most likely want to look more closely at the program's effectiveness and its organizational seaworthiness. Because this process is a deeper analysis, it is more time intensive. Foundations bereft of much staff often engage a philanthropic advisor or consultant. Individuals with donor-advised funds who value additional expertise beyond that offered through their giving vehicle could also seek this kind of research. A due diligence report gives the donor a clearer look behind the façade of the nonprofit to avoid surprises or fatal flaws.

The checklist for due diligence includes the following:

- Verification of 501(c)(3) tax-exempt status
- Most recent 990 form
- Mission statement
- Annual report
- Current operating budget
- Audited financials (if they have them—not all do)
- Board of directors: their qualifications, diversity, participation
- Qualifications of staff: knowledge in service area, nonprofit experience
- Plan for the year, with specific goals and objectives
- Analysis of overall program effectiveness
- Method of evaluation for proposed project
- Listing of current major donors
- Plan for sustaining funding for the project beyond this grant

Larger gifts, certainly those of $100,000 or more, demand a full-scale evaluation. Foundation staffs obviously fulfill this role. However, for foundations with sparse staffing or for individuals, a trusted philanthropic advisor or consultant would most likely provide this. Issues to address in a deeper due diligence process include, in addition to the above:

- "Environmental scan" to examine the climate and context of the program, and other groups providing similar services
- Examination of purpose and strategy
- Business plan
- Legal issues affecting the donor and recipient
- Human resources issues
- Sources of support, including individuals, foundations, corporations, churches, in-kind, endowment, service fees, earned income, government
- Longer-term sustainability of fund development
- Marketing strategies
- Organizational history
- Investigation of any potential liabilities jeopardizing success
- Output metrics: ratio of cost of services provided to number of individuals served
- Outcomes-based evaluation: building evaluation component into the grant to track effectiveness

A number of organizations provide assessment of nonprofits in general, although few specialize in analysis of faith-based organizations. Among those offering various kinds of assessment are GuideStar, Better Business Bureau Wise Giving Alliance, Evangelical Council for Financial Accountability, American Institute of Philanthropy, Ministry Watch, and Charity Navigator. They use different criteria for rating organizations, but many draw on information from an organization's 990 forms. Some focus on compliance issues, while others examine an organization's financials. Taken in context, each approach is useful in gleaning information about a potential grantee in a snapshot based on their previous year's performance. This kind of analysis is dispassionate and helpful in comparing one nonprofit to another. Because of its nature, however, this kind of rating system does not give a satisfactory in-depth analysis for an individual donor.

Calvin Edwards, who has garnered experience with his own philanthropic advisory firm, issues a note of caution:

> Of necessity, all these tools are limited in *scope* and heavily weighted toward financial analysis. For example, none evaluates a charity's marketing, public relations, or communication effectiveness. Management quality is not reviewed and is often inferred from financial results. They are also limited in *discernment*. Clinical, objective, numerically oriented reports cannot get at the heart of an organization. They can miss issues pertaining to the stage, location, or obstacles a ministry may face. . . . None of these tools accomplishes program evaluation. To know that a ministry only spends 3% on fundraising and

7% on general and administrative costs still leaves the question unanswered: How effective are the programs that receive 90% of the funding?[6]

Philanthropic advisors are useful in performing the due diligence inquiries that gifts of more than $10,000 should have. Martin C. Lehfeldt, president of the Southeastern Council of Foundations in Atlanta, says, "The growing number of faith-based and community nonprofit organizations often makes it difficult for busy donors with no staff assistance to discern which potential recipients are best able to achieve positive change and measurable results. However, local community foundations and professional philanthropic advisors can be good resources for this kind of assistance."[7] But there is no substitute for seeing the operation firsthand, particularly in assessing smaller, neighborhood-based, faith-based organizations, to get an accurate reading on what a group does, how effective it is, and whether or not the leader and the program are worthy of investment.

three

Evaluating Programs

The present climate of philanthropy increasingly demands that grant recipients demonstrate their effectiveness. A great chasm separates good intentions from good results, and it is appropriate to expect that grantees show their work's value. A growing number of sociological studies have documented results of religiously based programs, but few faith-based organizations have been studied individually. The programs that have been the objects of such inquiry have established benchmarks against which similar organizations can be compared. But the field is not yet populated with enough research to establish ironclad standards on effectiveness for FBOs as a whole. They require individual evaluation of their own merits.

But that does not mean that a private donor or a foundation must give blindly. President Reagan's arms policy of "trust but verify" applies here as well. Asking the right questions before making a grant is important. Many leaders of faith-based groups are visionaries, but not all can translate the vision into a strategy and measurable results. To ascertain the quality of the nonprofit's approach, questions from Peter Drucker's "Self-Assessment Tool" are helpful.[8] After adapting the language slightly for use with FBOs, questions to ask are:

- What is your mission?
- Whom do you serve?
- What do the participants value?
- What are your outcomes?
- What is your plan?

Leaders of faith-based organizations who can give a cogent answer to each of these questions have probably analyzed the program side of their organizations. Clearly articulated goals and demonstrated outcomes distinguish effective work.

The differentiation between outputs and outcomes is important. Consider a church-based after-school mentoring program. When staff is asked what they do, they respond that they provide mentors for twenty-five at-risk youth who come for two hours every week. That explains how often they provide the activity and the number of people involved—the output. But the outcome, the net result of that activity, is expressed through changed behavior or attitudes of the participants, or in their improved knowledge or competence. These could be measured in youngsters' higher grades, fewer disciplinary infractions at school, higher graduation rates, more parole appointments kept, decreased gang activity, or fewer teen pregnancies. An output uses activity to quantify what an organization does; an outcome expresses the difference a program makes in the lives of the people served.

 There is a big difference between handing out sandwiches to homeless people under the bridges and helping them to leave homelessness altogether.

Using that logic, a donor can scrutinize the field of grantees and distinguish between the groups that have good intentions but merely alleviate symptoms and those groups that address root causes and make lasting change. There is a big difference between handing out sandwiches to homeless people under the bridges and helping them to leave homelessness altogether. The most effective homeless shelters offer a drug treatment program, as addiction is often a root cause of homelessness. The most effective transitional living shelters offer continuing education for completing a high school equivalency degree or English as a second language as well as character development programs. Welfare-to-work programs that teach job skills and help place graduates in employment are doing good work, but if they provide mentors who teach life skills while strengthening the participants spiritually, they can effect transformation.

The same logic distinguishes between programs for immigrants that give them emergency groceries and those that provide them with entrepreneurial skills to become self-supporting. Programs for at-risk youth that include strategies to reach the parents as well as the youngsters can more effectively stabilize the situation that produces the child's need. Faith-based organizations offering a food pantry and clothes closet without asking the recipients any questions produce less lasting change than those that offer clients the option of entering a job-readiness program with a mentor. If a program's explicit goal is to end the dependency of the people served and to equip them for productive lives, it will more likely produce these results over time.

The "Faith Factor"

What is the faith distinction that justifies giving to faith-based organizations? Is there truly a "faith factor" that renders such work particularly effective? Byron Johnson has researched that question exhaustively.[9] In his study "Objective Hope: Assessing the Effectiveness of Faith-Based Organizations," Johnson reviews the literature on the efficacy of faith. He looks first at "organic religion," that experienced by those raised in the church who attend weekly services with their families as adults and experience faith as an ongoing part of life. He differentiates between "organic religion" and "intentional religion," that which one experiences in entering a program for a specific purpose. After scrutinizing nearly eight hundred studies, most published in the last few years, Johnson concludes that the "faith factor," whether organic or intentional, does change lives.

 Byron Johnson's report presents overwhelming evidence that faith is an important factor in health, and in reducing drug use and crime.

He writes, "[H]igher levels of religious involvement are associated with: reduced hypertension, longer survival, less depression, lower levels of drug and alcohol use and abuse, less promiscuous sexual behaviors, reduced likelihood of suicide, lower rates of delinquency among youth, and reduced criminal activity among adults." The report presents "overwhelming evidence that higher levels of religious involvement and practices make for an important protective factor that buffers or insulates individuals from deleterious outcomes."[10]

For example, Johnson investigated the relationship between religious commitment and drug use of urban teens, and concluded that religious low-income teenagers were 17 percent less likely to use marijuana and 6 percent less likely to use hard drugs than their inner-city teenage neighbors.[11] Highly religious youth in inner-city neighborhoods were less likely to use drugs than non-believing middle-class kids in the suburbs. Sociologist John DiIulio concludes, "[I]n both organic and in intentional religion, there is objective hope for improving Americans' life prospects, especially among the children, youth, and families who number among our most truly disadvantaged fellow citizens."[12]

Documented Results

Drug addiction cripples entire pockets of our cities, particularly since the advent of crack cocaine. When Teen Challenge claimed a 70 percent success rate for people leaving drug addiction, government officials doubted the claim's veracity. A study sponsored by the U.S. Department of Health, Education and Welfare in 1975 concluded that Teen Challenge's actual success rate was 86 percent.[13] Subsequent studies in 1994 and 1999 have verified these results, still apparent in graduates of the program as long as thirteen years after leaving treatment.[14] Participants who stayed in the program for a full year had a higher rate of success than those who left earlier, indicating that transformation is a process, not an event. With 130 Teen Challenge centers in the United States and 250 more throughout the world, it is one of the premier organizations moving people out of addiction into productive lives.

Prison Fellowship International works with offenders to significantly reduce their likelihood of committing crimes and returning to prison. In Texas, Iowa, Kansas, and Minnesota, its program, InnerChange Freedom Initiative, has created a prison-within-a-prison where, for eighteen months before their release, volunteer participants are fully immersed in scriptural study, mentoring, education, job preparation, and reconciliation with victims. The program also provides mentoring after participants are released. Byron Johnson's study documents that of those men who completed the program, 17.3 percent were rearrested within two years compared to 35 percent of the control group. Only 8 percent went back to prison.[15]

 Faith-based prison programs have cut recidivism to 8 percent, while some mentoring programs boost performance of at-risk youngsters across the board.

In Texas, Bridges to Life puts victims of crime face-to-face with offenders in prison. Over the course of twelve weeks, victims of crime volunteer from local churches to form small groups with perpetrators of crime to wrestle with guilt, forgiveness, and reconciliation. A widow whose husband was murdered, or the father of a child who overdosed on drugs may sit across the table from a convicted murderer or drug dealer. The conversations go deep and can be raw, but they put a face on crime for the prisoners, who vow not to commit another act like the one for which they were imprisoned. Five years into the program, founder John Sage has graduated his one thousandth inmate and has reduced the percentage of returning prisoners from the national average of 50 percent or more to 8 percent, as documented by statistics of the Texas Department of Criminal Justice.

Mentoring at-risk children can have a profound impact on their behavior and academic achievement. Kids Hope USA has adopted a highly effective one-on-one strategy. It pairs one church with one school and one adult with one grade-school child. A recent study of participating principals and teachers indicates that 100 percent of the children participating improved in their motivation for schoolwork, and that after one year, the academic achievement of 95 percent of the pupils was rated "good" or "excellent." The academic improvement is even higher in the second year of mentoring. Many of the requests for Kids Hope USA mentors are now coming from public school principals. The program has now been successfully replicated in 217 partnerships in twenty-six states across the country, providing mentors for 3,800 public elementary school children.[16]

In Memphis, the Urban Youth Initiative has trained and deployed 107 youth workers in the middle and high schools, saturating those with the highest concentration of at-risk youth. The program regularly involves at least five thousand kids, and interacts at some level with ten thousand. The youth workers, many from disadvantaged backgrounds themselves, serve as assistant guidance counselors and trou-bleshooters in school, and offer spiritual nurturing outside of school at local churches. The Wilder Foundation surveyed the students, their parents, and school officials, and documented changed attitudes.[17] Eighty-four percent of the students have a greater sense of hope in their ability to influence their future; 81 percent rely more on their faith in God in making decisions; 75 percent say their awareness of right and wrong is clearer; academic achievement improved for 69 percent; conflict resolution using peaceful means improved for 67 percent.

For profiles of other faith-based organizations that demonstrate documented success, see the companion volume to this guide, *Street Saints: Renewing America's Cities* (Templeton Foundation Press, 2004). Contact information for all the groups is available at the Web site www.streetsaints.com.

 Beware: demanding too much evaluation can cripple an organization's mission.

Potential donors should be aware that there are a bewildering number of approaches to evaluation. Full-scale sociological studies executed externally by aca-demic institutions and professional researchers with control groups are high-budget items. Expecting that kind of research from most faith-based organizations is not realistic. They have neither the staff nor the expertise or budget to comply. Demand-ing too much from them in evaluation can deflect them from their mission, warns Doug Easterling in his article "The Dark Side of Outcome Evaluation." He writes: "Evaluating the precise effect of a program requires not only a significant outlay of resources (e.g., funding staff time, client time) but also a shift in the organization's focus [from] creating change to creating knowledge. When foundations overpromote outcome evaluation, it may appear to their grantees that they are placing the evalua-tion process above the value-adding process."[18] In other words, demanding too much evaluation can cripple an organization's mission.

Outcomes-Based Evaluation

Faith-based groups often resist the demand for evidence of their effectiveness. Tom McCallie of the Maclellan Foundation says, "The frustrating thing is that they focus on activities and think if they just did their activities more often, they could do more in Kingdom value. I have resistance with Christian organizations that say you can't measure the Holy Spirit. I say I think you can. We can measure conversion rates, church growth, and any number of things that indicate he is there." McCallie goes on to say, "We believe theologically that anything that happens occurs in three worlds—the physical world, the emotional world, and the spiritual world. And we may not always be able to measure all, but we ought to be able to measure one."

If leaders of faith-based groups protest that they cannot measure their outcomes, consider suggesting this tool: "Outcomes-Based Evaluation" sharpens the focus of managing programs while equipping leaders to document their results. This approach is gaining recognition as a useful tool for faith-based organizations because it allows for individualized evaluation criteria in assessing effectiveness.[19] Participants trained in this approach build a logic model to express the purpose of their program, identify the outcomes it is intended to produce, identify criteria for measuring outcomes, and then use the criteria to track effectiveness over time. Outcomes are expressed as changes or improvements in behavior, skills, knowledge, or attitudes that result from the program.[20]

 "Anything that happens occurs in three worlds—the physical world, the emotional world, and the spiritual world. We ought to be able to measure one."

Workshops immerse participants in these concepts, while guiding them through the process of applying them to their own organization. Participants develop a tailor-made plan for evaluating one of their programs. Claudia Horn, Pat Fagan, and Calvin Edwards explain in their Heritage Foundation "Backgrounder" that participants:

- Compose a purpose statement for their program.
- Identify what the organization does, for whom, and for what outcome or benefit.
- Develop a "logic model" that identifies the program's outcomes, how these outcomes are measured (indicators), and to whom the indicators apply.
- Decide what data sources will be used to measure these indicators, at what point this data is collected, and what goals the program expects to achieve for its clients.[21]

The analysis identifies not the services delivered (outputs), but the difference they make in the lives of the people who are served (outcomes).

 Outputs tell you what services a program delivers. Outcomes tell you what difference they make in the lives of the people served.

Sometimes one must simply take a lofty goal and tether it to practical demonstrations of its realization. A fatherhood program, for example, has as its mission to "help fathers turn their hearts to their children," but measuring success in those terms is difficult. After going through the training and receiving some coaching, the program's leaders defined measurable success in the number of hours a father spent with his child and the number of child-support payments he made on time. Both of these quantifiable changes reflect a father's changed heart, linking reformed attitudes to altered behavior.

Or consider drug rehabilitation. Outcomes-Based Evaluation methodology set four benchmarks for participants that demonstrate and solidify their progress in leaving drugs:

1. Refrain from using heroin for one year.
2. Establish a commitment to a heroin-free lifestyle.
3. Develop a plan of action to take control of their lives.
4. Engage in reconciliation with others in their lives that have been harmed by their addiction.

Benchmarks like these allow leaders to manage participants through the process, making adjustments if necessary while monitoring and tracking their progress.[22] This approach establishes not only a finish line for the leaders of faith-based organizations, but also markers along the way. Groups using this tool can improve their performance en route because they have a way to evaluate their success. They can also apprise donors of their progress because meeting benchmarks demonstrates tangible improvement.

Calvin Edwards confirms, from his own experience of interfacing with donors and FBOs, that using Outcomes-Based Evaluation as a management tool sharpens a group's focus and moves performance to a higher standard. He advocates that donors build in 5–10 percent of a grant for evaluation and encourage their grantees to utilize this process. It may be a challenge to persuade overstretched leaders who often work with a minimal staff to put in the time and effort to follow through with a process like this. But if donors want to see demonstrated outcomes, they should consider making money available for personnel training and time to utilize the Outcomes-Based Evaluation technique. Because so many faith-based organizations tend to be individualized in what they provide, the approach outlined above may be a flexible response to their need for accountability without crippling the organization under scrutiny.

four

What to Look For
Signs of Health

After years of grant-making experience with the Bradley Foundation that took him to a number of smaller effective grassroots organizations, Bill Schambra became disenchanted with the current juggernaut toward metrics and "scientific evaluation." He said in *Philanthropy* magazine:

> Community activists champion "participatory evaluation," while wealthy entrepreneurs are drawn to "social return on investment." Other programs taking the field include Patton's utilization-focused evaluation, Stufflebeam's decision/accountability-oriented evaluation, Scriven's goal-free evaluation, Shadish's needs-based evaluation, and Norton and Kaplan's balanced scorecard measurement-based management approach. Small wonder that a recent survey of philanthropic leaders by the Center for Effective Philanthropy concluded, "each foundation has developed its own combination of metrics independently, described in different language, and applied in different ways."[23]

Instead, Schambra advocates "a more intuitive style of grant making based on practical wisdom and keen observations close to home." He encourages donors not to overlook some of the smaller faith-based organizations in their own backyard, for whom a less formal approach to evaluation is fully sufficient. He has ruffled the feathers of some in the professional philanthropic community by advocating a common-sense "eyeballing" of local groups. Simply go and see them, he says. Find out if they are doing what they say. Look to see if they are busy and responsive to real needs in the neighborhood. Check for evidence they have earned the respect of the locals by noticing signals like the absence of graffiti. See if the operation is run frugally: duct tape and well-used, mismatched furniture can be healthy signs of a modest budget. Most importantly, are they the right people doing the right things? If so, they are likely to be a good investment. "While the largest foundations continue to tie themselves in knots in the Evaluation Wars," Schambra concludes, "smaller foundations [and individuals] are free to undertake the deliberate, cumulative, intuitive process of mapping networks of effective grassroots groups in their own backyards, compiling over time their own checklists of effectiveness, based on their own local experiences. Measurable outcomes are not substitutes for this deeper wisdom."[24]

Signs of Health

The best of faith-based work in America today goes beyond giving alms—it goes deep enough to transform human lives. While it may appear compassionate to give a homeless person a handout, if it perpetuates a destructive lifestyle driven by addiction, giving indiscriminately can actually damage him or her. Bob Coté at Step 13 in Denver calls the government SSI checks mailed to homeless alcoholics "suicide on the installment plan," because some men drink themselves to death on the days the checks arrive. Addressing root problems may entail a long and sometimes painful process. The best of faith-based organizations work at a level that produces fundamental change and lasting results. Because faith can change motivation, it can cure stubborn social maladies that have not responded to secular remedies.

Experience with hundreds of faith-based organizations that provide social services reveals several consistent characteristics. These are traits to look for:

- Effective faith-based organizations deal with root causes.
- Their responses are flexible and personalized.
- They are rooted in the neighborhoods of the people they serve.
- They provide a hand up, which is more effective than giving a handout.
- They enfold the people they serve into supportive communities.
- They foster healthy, whole families.
- They work relationally, and go deep enough to change lives.
- They treat people with dignity.

 Because faith can change motivation, it can cure stubborn social maladies that have not responded to secular remedies.

Faith-based organizations have one particular strength in their highly relational approach. The foot soldiers in the armies of compassion, today's "little platoons," provide a human contact that a large, impersonal institution cannot. Because their leaders work face-to-face, there is a dynamic of personal change. And personalized solutions can be tailor-made to fit the need. Oftentimes the leaders of faith-based organizations come from the population they are serving. A former heroin addict can be extremely persuasive when he tells an addict that he can leave drugs, because he has done so himself. A former welfare recipient is an effective job coach for a neighbor on the same journey toward productivity. A former gang member is an effective mentor for youngsters endangered by gang participation. And while the cultural gap between donors and people with backgrounds like these is great, it is worth bridging the gap to see what they do. The savvy of these street saints qualifies them as experts in their field.

Penetrating Questions to Ask

Ask some penetrating questions in considering up front what kind of organizations to select for a contribution. In looking at faith-based organizations, particularly the neighborhood-based variety, practical signs of health indicate a likelihood of effectiveness. Questions to ask that will go beneath the surface to get to the essence include:

Are they providing a social service or are they transforming lives?

Freddie Garcia, a former heroin addict who has helped more than thirteen thousand people leave drugs through Victory Fellowship in San Antonio, says, "You can take a drug addict off drugs and you've got a reformed junkie. Or you can change his heart and you've got a transformed human being." Only faith-based organizations can claim this distinctive mission, so assessing their success in accomplishing transformation is crucial.

Do the leaders meet the "zip code" test?

Bob Woodson of the National Center for Neighborhood Enterprise has sought out and trained several hundred grassroots leaders all over the country. The most effective among them, he says, live in the same zip code as the people they serve. John Perkins, the father of the Christian Community Development movement, has reached the same conclusion, and calls for leaders to relocate into the same neighborhood as their outreach.

Are they connected to other local providers or operating in isolation?

If the group is part of a broader strategy and cooperates with other like-minded organizations, it is less likely to duplicate services. A surprising number of FBO leaders toil unaware that two blocks away someone else is trying to do the same thing, and that they would be stronger working together.

Do they ask something in return from the recipients?

When people in need walk into Aldine Y.O.U.T.H. in Houston, Sylvia Bolling asks them what they can do to serve in her neighborhood center. Parents who want Christmas presents for their kids help put up decorations first. A woman who wants groceries may sweep the floor before she goes to the food pantry. This approach values people enough to preserve their dignity by letting them participate through something they can offer. Bolling's approach mirrors the "sweat equity" of people who help build the Habitat for Humanity home into which they move.

Are they responding entrepreneurially to support themselves?

Innovative nonprofits devise ways to generate revenue, which ensures more stability. The unlikely workforce of handicapped adults at Brookwood Community in Texas produces pottery, plants, and silk-screened cards in micro-enterprises on site. The work they do serves as both therapy and education, and it gives the participants the satisfaction of meaningful productivity while generating income that covers a fourth of the community's $9.5 million budget.

Does their work go deep enough to accomplish lasting change?

Random acts of kindness do not necessarily change lives. Volunteers for Kids Hope USA are required to commit to weekly mentoring sessions with grade school pupils for at least one full year, and many continue for several years, entering into relationships with the parents and siblings as well. Friends of the Children in Portland, Oregon, pairs full-time paid young adult mentors with at-risk youngsters for ten years. "We believe in relentless effort," says Friends of the Children director Doug Stamm. "We will not allow kids to fail."

If the program is commodities-based, is there a link to relationship?

A program that merely distributes clothes or food without offering an opportunity to meet spiritual needs as well does not meet its fullest potential as a faith-based group. Economic and spiritual poverty often have a linkage, according to John Perkins, who has spent a lifetime working with poverty issues. He believes that relationship can be a healing factor in ameliorating both. The most effective FBOs understand that addressing physical and spiritual needs is much more likely to result in lasting change.

Are volunteers used effectively to accomplish the mission?

One of the indicators of health in a nonprofit is a hub of motivated volunteers who are willing to work alongside the staff. Particularly with faith-based groups, they reflect the degree of commitment shared.

Do the leaders have moral integrity and a teachable spirit?

Hugh Maclellan, who heads the Maclellan Foundation, says, "Most of the worst mistakes we made in granting were to people who weren't humble, weren't teachable, and weren't accountable to their board." Rick Wiederhold of the Elizabeth Brinn Foundation adds, "There are some spiritual charlatans out there." He recommends taking the time to get to know the leaders well, because it is worth finding the truly good ones.

Is the board of directors adequate to the task and engaged?

One of the particular soft spots for faith-based organizations is weak boards. Few boards reflect a broad reach into the community, making them incapable of engendering necessary support. Seldom do board members of FBOs have training to fulfill their roles well.

Peer-to-Peer Advice

Tom McCallie, who has guided the Maclellan Foundation in Chattanooga as its executive director for many years, has sorted through innumerable proposals for grants. He spells out the characteristics the foundation seeks in faith-based organizations:

> We look for Godly leadership. In the long run, the leadership is going to define whatever happens. We want to see that they are ministering where the action is, where God is already at work. We want to see them on a war footing—focused, ready to move. We don't want to see them foolishly spending money on things that are not needed. We want to see them innovating, always checking what they are doing and making corrections. We look for an organization that is growing, not one that is stagnant. We want to see an organization that stresses accountability and not necessarily accounting. We want one with a track record—we want to know they have done something well in the past. We want an organization that has very clear purposes and clear strategies, that knows what it is trying to accomplish and what it is measuring. They need to be able to balance the short-term and long-term tensions and give attention to what keeps them in business tomorrow as well as doing what's necessary today.[25]

A Note of Caution: Beware of Red Flags

Donors should be aware that not everything that calls itself faith-based is necessarily good. Soft spots in many faith-based groups merit caution. Beware of these red flags:

• *Groups that try to do too many things.* This is a common failing in faith-based organizations, which are needs-driven and often spread too thinly. They often lack focus.

• *Startups with no track record.* Their failure rate is very high. While providing seed money for a new endeavor can be innovative, more due diligence should establish the leader's credibility and credentials, as well as the probability of the plan's success.

• *The gap between proposals and reality.* Some organizations look terrific on paper but in actuality do not live up to what is portrayed. On the other hand, a proposal that is not written by a professional may not accurately portray exceptional work a grassroots group does. Get to know the organization firsthand on-site.

• *Programs trying to grow too big, too fast.* If the organization has a current budget of less than $100,000 and expects to grow to $750,000 next year without ever having made such a leap, the leaders are probably delusional. Sustained fund-raising is likely to be harder than they think.

- *Founder's syndrome.* Many founders of faith-based organization launch their work with passion and purpose but are not willing to step back and relinquish control when the work grows beyond their capabilities.

- *An organization with a weak board.* Beware if the board has three members of the founder's family and no visible reach outside the immediate community. The board's competency and engagement is crucial for a nonprofit's success.

- *Parachuting in outside solutions.* Whether suburbanites move into urban settings or Americans relocate to foreign countries, the likelihood of success is slim without indigenous leadership and local credibility.

- *Turf wars.* Do not underestimate the territorial imperative, which runs strong in the ministry world. Motivation by faith does not necessarily translate into mutual trust or cooperation with other groups, which are often seen as competitors.

- *Naïveté.* Some people are so heavenly minded that they are no earthly good. If they want to work with gang members, they need to understand reality. As Bob Woodson remarked, "We check for weapons. We may be spirit filled, but we ain't crazy."

five

Capacity Building
Leveraging Impact

Because the strengths of faith-based organizations are in the service area and the weaknesses are likely to be in the back office, investing in them strategically can bolster their competencies where most needed. Taking leaders who are passionately committed to their mission and trying to turn them into organizational grinds would be counterproductive. Their skill set lies elsewhere, driven by other interests. Unless, however, they acquire the skills or get outside help, they will never fulfill their potential. Perceptive donors have produced profound effects when their contributions include capacity building as well as financial support.

Faith-based groups are often "woefully underdeveloped organizationally," confirms Dr. Christine Letts, founder of Harvard University's Nonprofit Policy and Leadership Program. "Faith-based organizations have program competence, but they need core competencies beyond program, which is a challenge. They need fund-raising capacity, planning capacity, supervisory capacity, multi-site management, logistics, and human resources. They always have too little staff and they're undercapitalized."[26] Capacity building helps take these diamonds in the rough, hone their facets, and let them shine from the darkness they pierce.

 Capacity building helps take these diamonds in the rough, hone their facets, and let them shine from the darkness they pierce.

Increased capacity translates into changed lives, explains Jamie Levy, president of J.D. Levy & Associates and a faculty member at Indiana University in the Center on Philanthropy, The Fund Raising School, and the School of Public and Environmental Affairs. "The mission is the yardstick and capacity building is a means to realize greater portions of the mission. Organizational capacity building is expressed in organizational growth such as increased competence, effectiveness of programs, enhanced revenue streams, and the board's ability to lead." Building capacity allows groups to do what they do more competently and serve people effectively in ways that change more lives for the better. Greater capacity translates into improvement in attitude, knowledge, skills, behavior, or life condition of the people being served. Levy has trained hundreds of leaders of FBOs and, from this experience, concludes that the knowledge level of their boards limits many of them. He advocates a strategic investment in providing workshops for board development.

What Foundations Can Learn from Venture Capitalists

Christine Letts triggered discussion in foundation suites with her article "Virtuous Capital: What Foundations Can Learn from Venture Capitalists."[27] She argued in the *Harvard Business Review* that

> traditionally, foundations make grants based on their assessment of the potential efficacy of a program. Although that approach creates an incentive for nonprofits to devise innovative programs, it does not encourage them to spend time assessing the strengths, goals, and needs of their own organizations. Thus they often lack the organizational resources to carry out the programs they have so carefully designed and tested. Foundations need to find new ways to make grants that not only fund programs but also build up the organizational capacities that nonprofit groups need for delivering and sustaining quality.[28]

Letts suggests that foundations consider the following questions for assessing their own giving, taking a page from venture capital ideas, and relating them to capacity building:[29]

- Will our grants give nonprofits the organizational support necessary to achieve program goals?
- What internal capacity do we need to build organizational strength at the nonprofit?
- Is our grant portfolio too heavy on program innovation at the expense of organization building?
- Are we close enough to nonprofits to help them build organizational strength?
- Are there ways for us to experiment with some new types of grants?

Also addressing capacity building in the *Harvard Business Review*, Michael E. Porter and Mark Kramer argued in "Philanthropy's New Agenda: Creating Value" that "satisfied with their historic agenda of doing good, too few foundations work strategically to do better. The time has come to embrace a new agenda, one with a commitment to creating value."[30] Porter and Kramer lament that only 2.2 percent of foundation grants are designed to improve grantees' performance. They contend that foundations that provide capacity building can leverage a return on dollars by a factor of fifty to one hundred.

Capacity building can have a profound effect on an organization if undertaken when it has reached a minimum threshold of experience but before it becomes so established that it feels it has nothing to learn. Finding the right partners at the right phase of their development determines everything, according to the Milton S. Eisenhower Foundation. From 1990 to 2000, this operating foundation worked with eighty grassroots inner-city nonprofits to expand their capacity. According to the foundation's president, Lynn A. Curtis, the groups between three and five years old with budgets between $150,000 and $600,000 thrived most. "You have to have some capacity in order to use technical assistance and training," says Curtis. But "if they were too big or old, they had become fat and sassy and set in their ways and wouldn't listen to us" unless they were in dire straits. The most responsive, according to the *Chronicle of Philanthropy*, were those in the middle "that were growing and had a sense of momentum and were eager to acquire new organizational skills, all traits that made them rewarding to work with."[31]

 Foundations that provide capacity building can leverage a return on dollars by a factor of fifty to one hundred.

Grantmakers for Effective Organizations, which promulgates information on capacity building among its constituents, embodies a significant movement among philanthropists. A convergence of interest between the donor and the nonprofit leader must be found. Some donors ignore capacity building because they are too focused on getting every possible dollar into programs, viewing anything else as distracting or even wasteful. Many faith-based nonprofit leaders feel the same. It takes a particular kind of leader whose experience has led him or her to conclude he or she could use assistance in building capacity. As Letts remarked, "They're not all leaping to get this extra set of competencies."

From 1995 to 2000, the Mary Reynolds Babcock Foundation made 103 grants to strengthen a network of grassroots organizations in the South that were working to reduce poverty and racism. These capacity-building grants averaged $100,000 over three years and featured "peer-based learning." The foundation sponsored energizing gatherings for all the recipients to swap ideas with kindred leaders. Consequently, the foundation now encourages all applicants to consider their programmatic *and* organizational needs.[32]

Curriculum for Capacity Building

Research by the Center for Renewal indicates that faith-based organizations often need strengthening in the following areas. Strategic grants that tie multiyear operating grants to training or consultants who can offer this expertise multiply the effectiveness of FBOs.

- Management training
- Strategic planning
- Program design
- Replication of successful models/best practices
- Evaluation and outcomes measurement
- Personnel/human resources
- Board development
- Fund-raising
- Revenue-generating enterprises
- Grant management
- Accounting/bookkeeping
- Information technology
- Marketing and media
- Legal assistance

While nonprofit centers and organizations like the United Way offer training in a number of these areas, individualized attention tailor-made for FBOs, with regular follow-up, is far more effective.

The David and Lucile Packard Foundation has been building the capacity of the organizations it funds for more than fifteen years. The foundation lets the grantees decide what management issues they want to tackle rather than making recommendations. "If a grantee wants to work on board development, but it looks to us like they need to work on financial management, it's not about our priority, it's about theirs," says Barbara D. Kibbe, the director of Packard's Organizational Effectiveness and Philanthropy Program. "In our view, the bus has a route. It doesn't matter what stop you get on; it's eventually going to hit all the stops."[33] The foundation awards more than $8 million in such grants.

Carolyn Watson of the Rockwell Fund in Houston has led an initiative for leaders of "zip code ministries," which provide an umbrella for social services in regions of the city by pooling resources and volunteers from local churches. The Rockwell Fund issued a Request for Proposals to local ministries, looking for participants willing to enter a peer-learning network as part of a package that would include capacity-building training linked to three years of funding for operations. The project attempts to build not only the capacity of the individual ministries and their leaders, but to create a dynamism among them that will help them thrive long after the initial grant. Watson reports that many of the participants have been enthusiastic, although a few of them basically said, "Just send the check."

Because so much in the faith world is done on a shoestring, targeted capacity building can strengthen leaders who are otherwise limited by their budgets and their boards. The Rockwell Fund earmarked funds for FBO staff to attend training conferences not otherwise available to them. Other foundations have made grants specifically for new staff positions to help organizations grow to the next level of competency. There is sometimes resistance in FBOs because of the assumption that paying salaries commensurate with other nonprofits or having a fund-raiser on the staff is "unspiritual." But if an FBO is going to develop beyond the shoestring and duct-tape phase, some organizational capacity is necessary.

Leveraging Promise: The Maclellan Foundation

The Maclellan Foundation in Chattanooga has a long and distinguished history in funding Christian organizations. Hugh Maclellan, whose father began the foundation, has focused on finding "not only good works, but the best works." The foundation focuses on both domestic and international Christian organizations. Hugh Maclellan says that one of the most successful things the foundation has done for the groups is to fund targeted coaching sessions for the leadership. It sends the nonprofit executive, the chairperson of the board, and one key staff person to a trusted consultant for an intensive two-day coaching session. The nonprofit's leadership team examines its mission, programs, the board function, and results, utilizing questions like the Drucker Self-Assessment Tool. By taking the time to step back from the everyday tyranny of the urgent to focus on the essentials, the team makes major breakthroughs. In the past five years, the foundation has provided this opportunity for nearly one hundred organizations, averaging nearly twenty each year. Maclellan says, "We're stepping it up, because it's the best use of our funds we have."

Hugh Maclellan says that one of the most successful things the foundation has done for the groups is to fund targeted coaching sessions for the leadership.

The foundation has also funded recruiting, development, organizational consulting, and program development. They ask the organizations to cover half the cost to guarantee their full participation. McCallie says the foundation prefers to work with organizations that have demonstrated success rather than with startups. "You have to know your expertise. Ours is trying to find an organization that has a product with a little bit of a proven track record, but now needs to go big. We can take that type of organization and make it successful." Both Maclellan and McCallie agree that capacity building has added significant value to their grant making. "When we look back over twenty to thirty years of granting, probably our most leveraged dollars have been with consulting help," says McCallie. "We consistently get that back from organizations."

Social Capital plus Competence: Fred Smith

Fred Smith, who convenes The Gathering (www.thegathering.com), a group of Christian donors, also runs the Fourth Partner Foundation in Tyler, Texas. There, he oversees granting to a variety of faith-based and community initiatives. Even though he is a strong advocate for faith-based organizations, he does not give them preferential treatment when they apply for funding from the foundation. "I don't look for faith-based organizations. I look for competence," says Smith. "I target organizations that have a capacity for growth."

With a staff of seven, the Fourth Partner Foundation formulates a strategy for removing barriers to achieve the nonprofit's mission. They direct much of their effort toward strengthening the organization. Smith explains, "Ideas tend not to turn into reality without organizations. Our foundation is set up to help other organizations get results. We build on islands of health and strength. We work with those who are receptive. And we only work where, if it works, it will make a difference." His staff brings strong nonprofit management experience to the table, and they work hands-on with grantees to solve problems and build capacity. For some, they help prepare the budget; for others, they send members of the board of directors to a workshop, or pick up the salary for a necessary executive position.

 "We want to be a partner. We bring money, counsel, and connections to the deal."

Ron Gleason explains, "We can teach groups to be intentional about how to get where they want to go." The foundation chooses its grantees with an eye toward a long-term relationship, often spanning multiple years. Over several years of collaboration, they can "teach a visionary leader how to sustain and inform his vision," says Dawn Franks. The team brings significant "social capital" to the task from a long history in the community. As Smith puts it, "We want to be a partner. We bring money, counsel, and connections to the deal."

The Fourth Partner collected ten years of financial history for one organization into a spreadsheet. This overview then enabled leaders to spot patterns and readjust their strategy. The foundation helped an Anglo church redesign its outreach programs to meet new demands in its changing community. In tandem with shifting demographics, the church initiated an after-school program and clinic, thereby meeting the needs of the neighborhood and reenergizing the church. The foundation also funded a staff member for Habitat for Humanity to increase the number of houses built, the number of volunteers, hours of construction, and dollars raised. These strategic interventions by the foundation increased the capacity of their grantees, leveraging their effect in the community.

Entrepreneurial Skills: David Weekley

Some donors, like Houston's David Weekley, support groups with time and talent in addition to funding. A successful entrepreneur in the building business, Weekley devotes half his time and income to the support of forty to fifty charitable causes, many of them Christian. Because he can give his entrepreneurial talent, he selects eight to ten organizations to work with in a given year, interacting personally with the leaders to hone strategic plans, tighten management, and accelerate progress. "As an entrepreneur, I am interested in growth and doing more rather than maintaining the status quo," Weekley says. "The first thing I want to see is whether they are efficient and effective. I look to see how a gift from me could leverage their current operations and create ten times or one hundred times the value. I look to see where I can add value to their organization from my own skill set and time, as well as my dollars."

 "I look to see where I can add value to their organization from my own skill set and time, as well as my dollars."

Weekley asks hard questions about results and helps the faith-based groups formulate measurements of their progress. Sometimes he pays for outside professionals. "The leaders might say we can't afford a fund-raising consultant and I'll say you can't afford not to. So I'll give them a grant to do that." He has funded a direct mail consultant for one group, and picked up two years' salary for a computer expert for another. For another organization, he paid for a firm's nationwide search for a high-quality, upper-level employee. Weekley insists on excellence. He says, "If we don't hold them to the same standards as we would in business, in terms of professionalism, or proficiency or efficiency, we are doing them a disservice. Because if we really want God's kingdom to be here, we need to have the same kind of standards of excellence as we do in anything else."

 "If we don't hold them to the same standards as we would in business, in terms of professionalism, or proficiency or efficiency, we are doing them a disservice. Because if we really want God's kingdom to be here, we need to have the same kind of standards of excellence as we do in anything else."

Building Capacity across the Country

Recognizing the untapped potential of many faith-based organizations, Pew Charitable Trusts has embarked on an ambitious plan to strengthen and support providers of faith-based social services, particularly those serving distressed urban communities. FASTEN (Faith and Service Technical Education Network) has compiled research on best practices nationwide and launched sophisticated online tools for practitioners. The Web site www.fastennetwork.org provides a wealth of information for leaders of FBOs, where they can log on to learn how to establish a 501(c)(3) organization, write a professional proposal to access funding, or download items like training manuals for mentoring programs. Rich resources on topics including youth entrepreneurship, crime prevention, and workforce development are now available, as are many others. Under Amy Sherman's competent leadership, information gleaned from successful faith-based programs all over America has been compiled, evaluated, and posted, and the library of materials is being augmented on a regular basis. Baylor University is conducting research to identify effective faith-based programs, while Harvard University's Hauser Center has convened selected mayors and their staffs to consider innovative models for citywide implementation. The Hudson Institute and the National Crime Prevention Council have been partners in developing Web materials, publications, and training events for this nationwide strategy to equip the nation's FBOs.

Generating Revenue: Social Entrepreneurs

Most nonprofit organizations struggle perpetually to raise funds. Some of the more entrepreneurially minded ventures have devised revenue-generating strategies to help cover the budget. One of the earliest pioneers in the field, the Roberts Enterprise Development Fund in California, strategically bolsters its grantees by offering both financial and intellectual capital. They have helped create "social purpose enterprises" for nonprofits, which offer, for example, positions where hard-to-place employees can be productive while earning something toward the cost of their care. (See www.redf.org.)

Other examples of revenue-producing enterprises with a social purpose:

• Pura Vida Coffee markets coffee grown in Latin America to Americans, utilizing the Internet. Because the business pays a living wage to the coffee growers, it adds value to their lives and turns the profits over to the ministry side of the operation in Costa Rica, which cares for street children and recovering drug addicts.

• Bob Coté at Step 13 in Denver puts the homeless men from his shelter to work as they leave drugs and alcohol. He deploys them in contract work including auto detailing, printing logos on T-shirts, or power washing houses and boats. The men learn the discipline of showing up for work on time and cooperating in a team, while producing more than half of the agency's $550,000 budget.

• Economic Opportunities in Memphis takes men in transition from prison or drug rehabilitation programs and offers them on-the-job training coupled with mentoring. The organization contracts with a local company to provide crate packing, pallet loading, or spray-painting, and works with the men to improve their skills and reliability. If they succeed, the men have a recommendation for future employment that helps to overcome their past.

• Jim Ortiz in Whittier, California, puts recovering drug addicts and ex-convicts to work repairing houses auctioned by the Department of Housing and Urban Development. The men gain carpentry and wiring skills while establishing a track record of gainful employment. Ortiz's ministry, My Friend's House, turns a profit of $10,000 on each of the houses, which helps cover the cost of the program.

 Social entrepreneurs are creating revenue streams while producing social purpose enterprises for the hard-to-employ.

Programs like these provide a profitable blend of ministry and business that builds up the capacity of the participants while stabilizing the organizations with revenue streams. Forward-thinking donors with an entrepreneurial bent could equip other faith-based organizations with models to fit their needs and aptitudes.

∷ six ∷

Ways to Give
Models in Action

If a donor is interested in the promise of faith-based organizations and is considering make a grant to one, what is the process? The first step is to determine where his or her passions lie and what kind of work is most appealing. The Giving Interest Inventory in the Donors' Toolbox at the back of this book can help narrow the field to groups that serve a specific population. Then one should look at the programs that various groups in the category offer and ascertain which of their strategies appears most sound. A look at their track record helps to determine their likelihood of success. Then a closer look at the finalist candidates is advisable in site visits, either done personally or by a staff member, or consultant. A philanthropic advisor can help narrow the field and evaluate potential grantees, assisting a donor through the process.

 A philanthropic advisor can help narrow the field and evaluate potential grantees.

After the site visits may come some interaction with the leadership of each of the finalist groups, possibly including participation in some of their activities to round out the portrait. This allows a dip into cultures the various groups embody and a taste of how they work. It is worth ascertaining whether a particular organization's style matches your interests. Some entrepreneurial donors prefer startups, while others like long-established organizations. Some givers prefer high-profile groups, while others like discovering diamonds in the rough. Some donors have looked around to see what exists in their own communities and have concluded they would rather start a new initiative themselves.

Finding out what an organization truly needs is important. It can be interesting to ask what the group would do if there were no constraints on additional funding.

What may emerge from the answer is a bigger and clearer vision than the proposal put forth, because so often applicants try to second-guess donors and ask for what they think they are likely to get.

Then a donor considers what to give, and how to give. It could be a gift of money, time, or talent. It might be stocks, a painting, a car, a boat, or a vacation house. It might mean putting business acumen to work in assisting a group. Consider which vehicle is most advantageous: an individual gift, or one made through a family foundation, community foundation, donor-advised fund, or charitable gifts fund. Each of these options has advantages and disadvantages, particularly as they relate to convenience and control. The tax and legal ramifications need to be considered, and are given a more detailed discussion in the Donors' Toolbox. Before a gift is given, the donor should consider what he or she wants to receive in return. Recognition for bettering the community? A name on a building or program to commemorate a family member? Reciprocity from another donor? Is the gift to serve as a signal to other donors to follow suit? Is it intended to be the beginning of a relationship with the organization? Or is it to be an anonymous gift?

With so many possibilities, it is helpful to learn from others who have grappled with the same questions. Organizations have sprung up to provide publications and facilitate peer learning for donors. Several organizations that have given thoughtful attention to the potential of faith-based organizations are worthy of special commendation, although there are many others doing admirable work.

The Gathering

The Gathering, under the leadership of Fred Smith, convenes meetings and programs for Christian donors who give at least $200,000 annually. The peer-to-peer aspect of this kind of organization is particularly valuable, say participating donors, who appreciate the experience of being with each other in a solicitation-free environment. Annual programs present firsthand experience from Christian donors as well as the expertise of nonprofit leaders who are invited to speak. People sharing a particular interest assemble for additional forums throughout the year. The Gathering offers programs and services specialized for individual donors, families, women, young givers, and foundations. What began in 1985 as a meeting of six people has grown to a network of some four hundred people throughout the country. The organization also publishes a newsletter for its membership. (See www.gatheringweb.com.)

Philanthropy Roundtable

The Philanthropy Roundtable, headed by Adam Meyerson, provides informative and thought-provoking programs for its members and produces a bimonthly magazine, *Philanthropy*. The Roundtable is a national association of about five hundred foundations, families, and corporate-giving programs committed to advancing freedom, opportunity, and personal responsibility in America and abroad. Though the Roundtable does not explicitly profess religious affiliation, it highly respects faith, and many of its members are actively involved in Evangelical, Catholic, and Jewish philanthropic causes. The organization convenes annual meetings in attractive locations with a high-powered array of speakers and experts, drawing foundation executives and talent from successful nonprofit initiatives. Affinity groups convene on issues including K–12 education, marriage and the family, environmental stewardship, and victory over terrorism. (See www.philanthropyroundtable.org.)

Generous Giving

As the largest and most active of the Christian foundations, the Maclellan Foundation is an invaluable resource, particularly for new donors. From its commitment to Christian giving, the foundation has birthed the Generous Giving initiative. It offers an array of publications, conferences, books, study guides, and online resources to foster generosity. Generous Giving focuses not only on donors, but also on ministry leaders, pastors, teachers, and professional advisors. In recognition of the need for better matchmaking between donors and programs, Daryl Heald has created the Generous Giving Marketplace, an online opportunity for Christian nonprofits to post proposals. Donors have access to an interest assessment tool to help narrow the focus of their interests and link them to proposals that are a good fit. The site does not prequalify the applications, but simply offers the service as a way for donors and applicants to make contact.

 "We're intentional about capitalizing our assets: relationships, experience, information, and knowledge."

Generous Giving also arranges conferences to share the wisdom gleaned from the foundation's involvement both domestically and internationally. As Heald explains, "Not everybody has fifty trips' worth of experience in Russia when they consider giving there." The consultations the foundation hosts bring together peer donors, for example, who have an interest in Africa, India, or China, and may take them to visit the countries together. Heald says, "We're intentional about capitalizing our assets: relationships, experience, information, and knowledge." The peer-to-peer approach shares the motivation, methods, and rewards other grant makers have experienced. (See www.generousgiving.org.)

Community Foundations

As community foundations rapidly spread throughout the country, their numbers approach one thousand, according to Helen Monroe, who has been instrumental in planting many of them. Donors wanting to concentrate on giving to the community without the administrative burden of setting up their own foundation have found this a welcome vehicle. These foundations aim to support broad, community-minded endeavors that serve the public good. (See www.cfamerica.org.) Historically, individual donors made a gift to a general fund to serve the community at large, leaving the particular designation of grants to the foundation's board. More recently, the trend toward donor-advised funds has grown to represent the largest share of community foundation giving.

The foundation supplies all the administrative services and provides a representative or department for donor services, which can offer information on grant possibilities. Some of the larger foundations also offer seminars and organize site visits for their donors. Monroe says that, in general, community foundation unrestricted funds do not support explicitly faith-based causes, but individual donors can recommend grants from their own donor-advised funds to organizations they choose. A recommendation is, however, just that: a recommendation. Community foundations each have their own unique character and may define their own parameters for determining which groups are serving the public purpose. In San Francisco and Denver, for example, the respective local community foundations declared the Boy Scouts' stance regarding homosexuality "discriminatory." In these two locations, therefore, the scouts may not receive unrestricted funding, but individual donors may still designate grants to them from their donor-advised funds.

 "The site visits were the most important part of the process, because it engaged the donors."

The Central Indiana Community Foundation offered its services to a group of donors who wanted to make grants to faith-based organizations. Local donors Don Palmer and Marty Moore asked fifteen people to give $20,000 each to establish a donor-advised fund within the community foundation. The group met regularly to map out their strategy, which included a survey of three neighborhoods to chart an overview of local churches and faith-based nonprofits. The donors visited the groups they were considering and, according to the foundation's executive vice president, Rosemary Dorsa, "The site visits were the most important part of the process, because it engaged the donors." The fund has given a series of smaller grants to test their strategy's success. They intend to launch a Christian Community Foundation in the future, building on the experience gleaned in this pilot project.

In Houston, entrepreneur Peter Forbes established the Equip the Saints fund to assist Christian ministries through the Greater Houston Community Foundation. With the help of a philanthropic advisor, he sought organizations poised to grow. He wanted to assist ministries that showed promise and an entrepreneurial bent, for whom a gift of $15–25,000 for two or three years would make a significant impact. He provided not only funding for the groups, but assistance through the advisor to help the recipients identify and meet strategic goals over the coming year. By combining the grant with personalized capacity building, he leveraged his investment by improving the grantees' effectiveness.

 By combining the grant with personalized capacity building, he leveraged his investment by improving the grantees' effectiveness.

National Christian Foundation: Christian Community Foundations

In 1982, Ron Blue, Larry Burkett, and Terry Parker founded the National Christian Foundation to serve donors who wanted to give to specifically Christian causes. After operating for a decade on a small basis, the foundation has now grown into an affiliation of fourteen local Christian Community Foundations with $350 million in assets and another dozen cities considering a similar initiative. An additional five Christian Community Foundations stand independently. NCF maintains a staff of thirty-five based largely in Atlanta to service their affiliates, whose leaders focus on serving individual donors in each of their fourteen cities. NCF granted $113 million in 2003, simultaneously providing for the network's services, including charitable gift planning services, administration, communication, assistance in handling complex gifts, and startup assistance to new foundations. (See www.nationalchristian.com.)

 "Most advice on giving starts with the assumption you want to keep everything. We try to turn the paradigm upside down, and focus on the giving."

Dave Worland, executive vice president of the National Christian Foundation, says its approach to philanthropy differs from most. "Most advice on giving starts with the assumption you want to keep everything and pass it on to the next generation," Worland explains. "Probably 90 percent of the information for donors deals with the techniques on how to keep what you have or avoid taxes. We try to turn the paradigm upside down, and focus on the giving. We believe God has raised up the provision, then He lets the person know what He wants to do. If they give then, it's a great, joyful place to be."

While donor-advised funds handle the bulk of giving, NCF also offers its donors "area of interest" funds—discipleship, education, evangelism, family, international, poor and needy, urban, and youth—to which they may designate a part of their giving. A board for each area allocates grants, typically $5,000, in response to a short, two-page request. Last year NCF distributed $800,000 this way, from their $113 million total.

Donor-advised funds can make recommended grants only to organizations whose values are consistent with the NCF statement of faith. Organizations with inconsistent values may not receive their funds. For example, the NCF would not approve hospitals that perform abortions, and they would urge donors wishing to support them to find another vehicle.

Jewish Philanthropy

Although comprising only 2 percent of the U.S. population, the six million Jews living here have founded and funded an expansive network of thousands of nonprofits and organizations. These organizations, some dating back to the country's earliest years, provide a broad range of services. Much of the giving occurs locally through synagogues, accompanied by community and national networks as well. Community organizations provide recreation and social networks, while cultural institutions build museums. United Jewish Communities is the umbrella organization for the local federations, which marshal an annual campaign. With assets of $8 billion, they distribute $800 million each year. The network of social and human service organizations includes Jewish Family and Children's Services, Jewish Vocational Services, and others that provide homes for the elderly, assisted living, and other services that are open to people of all faiths. Nationally, combined efforts help fund seminaries in the Orthodox, Conservative, Reformed, Reconstructionist, and other movements within Judaism. International funding supports the Jewish community abroad, both in Israel and elsewhere.

Jewish Philanthropy Partnership, run by Gary Tobin, convenes groups of major donors to develop partnerships and shared initiatives. The Jewish Funders Network also works with foundations to inform their giving. According to Tobin, "Most Jews, especially those giving the most money, tend to give to secular causes rather than to Jewish causes." Overall, higher education engenders the most support, followed by health-related concerns, and then arts and culture. Thousands of individuals and family foundations provide broad and generous support for a wide range of causes.

Kingdom Oil: Serving Donors and Faith Leaders

Lawyer Jay Bennett, after serving nearly two decades as the president of the Wallestad Foundation, decided that he wanted to create an additional vehicle for giving to churches and ministries. In his experience, pastors and nonprofit leaders found themselves competing rather than producing better projects and proposals together. Kingdom Oil, a Christian Community Foundation in the Twin Cities, began in 1997 with a new strategy. It offers donors the opportunity to give through donor-advised funds, for which they make recommendations, or to invest in a portfolio. Kingdom Oil offered the community a book profiling fifty local ministries as one of its first projects to lift the visibility of FBOs in the region and to offer a variety of opportunities to donors. Now, Web updates continue the project.

 "Find ministries which have relationships with the deep pain in a city. Resource them, honor them."

The innovative streak in Kingdom Oil has created a network of ministries and churches in nine portfolios: prayer and worship, information resources, leadership, youth and family, compassion and justice, Twin Cities partnerships, U.S. networks, international networks, and a general fund. Richard Coleman, the chief operating officer of Kingdom Oil, explains that fifty-nine leaders of these participating FBOs have signed a covenant to pray for each other, invest in each other's ministries, and seek to advance Kingdom purposes together. Kingdom Oil convenes the leaders to build relationships and strategize, with the hope that the participants will come up with new strategies for their sector. The foundation has assigned two shepherds to each portfolio group to facilitate the melding of interests. Organized intercessors pray for the participants as they work toward tangible plans together.

The relational piece of this foundation is a rare innovation. "The key to everything is relationally connecting resources to root causes," says Bennett. For others who would like to do the same, he advises: "Find ministries which have relationships with the deep pain in a city. Resource them, honor them, pray with them, invest in them as you are able, help build their capacity. And help them to know that they are a critically important piece of a bigger picture—a Kingdom picture."

Taking Personal Initiative: Foster Friess

Foster Friess often rode the train between New York and Wilmington. One day, as the train approached his home station, the trash-strewn lots and the vagrant men, many of whom obviously had substance abuse issues, caught his attention. At first, he made an effort to take on one man at a time as a personal project and encourage him along the path to sobriety and productivity. He learned of the issues they were dealing with by joining them for meals and sleeping the night in their shelter.

As he attempted to get churches involved, unenthusiastic responses stirred his conscience to provide a solution. He launched the He Is Pleased program, which began putting men to work who wanted to make a fresh start, paying them to clean up littered lots. To this day, He Is Pleased honors that focus by providing entry-level jobs to help the men back into the job market. The men benefit from the opportunity to practice showing up for work on time and completing tasks. This positive track record arms them as they seek employment elsewhere. Shelters, jails, and halfway houses further the ministry by referring men to He Is Pleased.

 He Is Pleased began putting men to work who wanted to make a fresh start, paying them to clean up littered lots.

Foster and Lynn Friess have now launched a one-on-one mentoring program in Phoenix's high crime area, Maryvale, where they are assembling a coalition of Christian organizations in an initiative called Desert Reach. They marshal caring Christian adults to mentor kids with unfulfilled promise, connecting them to the expertise and passions of the Boys & Girls Club, Young Life, Fellowship of Christian Athletes, the Hugh O'Brian Leadership Foundations, HOSTS, the Girl Scouts, the Boy Scouts, and The Best Friends Foundation.

Little League and Hope Academy: Bob Muzikowski

As one of Northwestern Mutual's top insurance executives, Bob Muzikowski grew tired of hearing about drugs and gangs in the inner city. He decided to help at-risk kids by establishing an inner-city Little League. He and his wife moved into Chicago's Cabrini Green area, and then to Chicago's West Side. They built a home where they reach out to the neighborhood kids on the ground floor, and live with their own seven children on the second and third floors of the house. "Probably two or three nights this week there will be four or five kids sleeping at our house. They knock at the door at ten o'clock and say, 'Coach, we're locked out.' I have a Bible on my desk, what am I supposed to say? Go somewhere else?"

After starting the Little League, Muzikowski bought a four hundred-acre farm in southern Illinois and founded a home for recovering prisoners and transitioning drug and alcohol addicts. Sixty-four men now live there, fishing out of the stocked catfish pond. Muzikowski funds the farm, for which Living Lights ministry provides the management. Muzikowski's sports programs have expanded to include soccer as well as Little League baseball, and tutoring has been added to improve the academic performance of the youngsters. Eleven hundred kids now participate in the sports and tutoring programs he has initiated. Muzikowski has sold half his business to devote more time to the projects he has launched, and he is recruiting others to invest in his ministries.

 Doing hands-on work in the inner city "is a lot more satisfying than going to seminars about it."

His most ambitious project, a Christian school for inner-city kids, Chicago
Hope Academy, opened its doors in the fall of 2004 with sixty youngsters and intends
to grow to six hundred students. Muzikowski believes that lasting change in the kids'
lives requires a full day's activities. "It's about teaching them truth. You need twelve
hours a day for that. I don't think any kid is unreachable. Some are hard, but all are
reachable." He challenges more donors to move into the cities to do hands-on work.
"It would change the country," he says. "And it's a lot more satisfying than going to
seminars about it."

Creating a Nonprofit Campus

A Midwest family foundation looked at the universe of giving possibilities and
decided to create an altogether new project. This family foundation purchased a
fourteen-acre cement-mixing dumpsite and restored it from an eyesore to its native
prairie beauty. Amidst tall grass in what was once an environmental graveyard, the
foundation planted a new one-stop campus for nonprofits serving the area's needy.

The family foundation created a business plan to erect buildings, provide the
infrastructure, and attract tenants to the campus. The campus can house up to twelve
nonprofits, and so far, three have moved in. They now provide a variety of services,
including funds for short-term emergency needs, a well-stocked food pantry, and a
community clothes closet. With the help of a philanthropic advisor, the community
association hired an executive director and set up a condominium community. Once
the first three service providers settled in, the community association mobilized relational care for the needy from local houses of worship. The synergy of the cooperating organizations in one location, now coupled with the human touch of *caritas* in
action, realizes the faith-inspired vision of a family.

Intersection with Business

Some business leaders have concluded they can do well by doing good. Providing funding for a faith-based organization can be good for business. David Oelfke
determined that turnover created the highest cost in the apartment complexes he
owned. Every time tenants left, the cost of renovation and lost rent cut into his bottom
line. By inviting in and supporting an apartment ministry that provided young cou-
ples to serve as social directors for the complexes, he invested in stability. As the cou-
ples got to know the tenants and promoted social get-togethers and Bible studies, the
neighbors' cohesiveness grew. Fewer tenants moved out as the relationships deep-
ened, which improved their quality of life and their spiritual lives, as well as earnings
for the owner.

Strategic gifts to the nonprofit sector can improve a business's position in rela-
tion to its competitors, say Michael Porter and Mark Kramer in the *Harvard Business*

Review.[34] Cisco Systems, for example, has invested in educational efforts to train computer network administrators, grooming high school students for attractive employment possibilities. By increasing the pool of well-trained talent, Cisco realizes both social and economic gains. Cisco has collaborated with some FBOs to provide such training. "By focusing on social needs that affect its corporate context and utilizing its unique attributes as a corporation to address them, Cisco has begun to demonstrate the unrealized potential of corporate philanthropy," Porter and Kramer conclude.[35]

 Partnering with an apartment ministry cut the rate of tenant turnover, improving their quality of life and their spiritual lives, as well as earnings for the owner.

Get Together: Entrepreneurs Brainstorm

Sometimes just putting the entrepreneurial energy of a group of businesspeople at the disposal of leaders of FBOs can spark a dynamic relationship. Paul McDonald in Houston concluded that the money he could give would eventually run out, but that his entrepreneurial vision would not. He collected a group of like-minded business leaders into the Get Together. In a freewheeling session every month, a few invited FBO leaders brainstorm with Christian executives, lawyers, computer experts, and multi-talents. The group visits the site of a different ministry every other month to experience the organization firsthand, then kicks into creative mode to solve problems for them. From the contacts and expertise of the group, the faith-based groups have paved parking lots, replaced kitchen equipment, installed air conditioners, launched micro-enterprises, and salvaged several hundred thousand dollars' worth of goods for FBOs. Members of The Gathering of Men, a partnering Christian businessmen's group, are exploring opportunities to engage relationally with at-risk kids in the groups with which they are involved. This model bridges the gap between their worlds.

A Nehemiah Strategy

A movement of faith-based intermediaries is growing throughout the country, building coalitions and coming up with strategies that encompass entire cities. Based on Nehemiah in the ancient Hebrew Scriptures, this approach assesses needs and then mobilizes workers at strategic points throughout the city to work together seamlessly for renewal. Jay Bennett of the Kingdom Oil Foundation says, "We use the Nehemiah example, where every family was assigned a section of the wall or a gate. They had a passion and the ability to build their section, but they kept their eyes and hearts on the welfare of the whole. They worked with micro passion and macro allegiance." Kingdom Oil collaborates with Urban Ventures and a number of other ministries in the Twin Cities to fulfill the Nehemiah vision.

 Intermediaries are linking civic, religious, educational, and business leaders in coalitions with the local police and city governments to transform communities.

Consider an example in Fresno, where a hospital sat ready to expand adjacent to a high-crime, low-income area full of recent immigrants. Rather than building a Taj Mahal with razor wire around it, the hospital collaborated with One by One Leadership, a local faith-based intermediary, which worked with the residents to form a grassroots neighborhood association and plan for the change together. The local schools participated too, offering classes to the parents, while the hospital offered training to the residents as potential new employees. The city put in sidewalks and streetlights, the police increased patrols, and crime dropped. The result benefited the hospital while sparking civic renewal for the community.

In other cities, including Pittsburgh, Memphis, Seattle, Phoenix, Chicago, Philadelphia, Knoxville, and two dozen others, faith-based Leadership Foundations are rallying workers to tackle citywide issues together.[36] Donors in each of the cities have funded initiatives that encompass civic, religious, educational, and business leaders in coalitions with the local police and city governments. In strengthening grassroots efforts and coming up with broader strategies, they have effectively reduced crime, improved the climate for business, and diminished gang violence while serving as catalysts for cooperation among churches and FBOs. Some donors who want to orchestrate a unified response are investing in such citywide efforts, forming grant-making foundations that work hand in hand with local intermediaries. The Hope Christian Community Foundation in Memphis is a good example of this kind of fruitful partnership, working hand in hand with the Memphis Leadership Foundation.

The Strengths of Intermediaries

Ferreting out individual faith-based groups may seem inordinately labor intensive, but working through local intermediaries can help. These groups usually bring knowledge and relationships in the faith sector to the table, along with firsthand experience with many of the local leaders. Nothing substitutes for lessons learned in the school of hard knocks, and most of the leaders of citywide intermediaries have countless bruises and battle scars. Their insights can prevent a donor from having the same experiences. Getting to know unfamiliar territory almost always results in paying what Daryl Heald calls "the dumb tax": the price of ignorance. Working through intermediaries can help lower the price. Because many intermediaries work cross-denominationally, they can reach a broad band of faith-based organizations. They are potential vehicles for capacity-building work, because it corresponds to the role they play for local FBOs.[37] And their position permits them to administer grants to other smaller organizations if so desired.

Suggestions from the Field

A number of donors and philanthropic advisors who have years of experience offer the following suggestions in making grants to faith-based organizations:

Consider multiyear grants.

Tom McCallie of the Maclellan Foundation likens grant making to dating. Total knowledge of the other person only comes after a couple of years of total honesty and transparency. In that time, trust facilitates the exchange of money as well as of knowledge, strategy, and relationships. Faith-based groups, so often under-resourced in all of these areas, will benefit from the infusion of these gifts. Multiyear grants allow an organization to practice better planning and to concentrate on what it is doing rather than on scouring the landscape for new support. A donor once told philanthropic advisor Calvin Edwards that he did not want a group to become dependent on him. "Who should they depend on, if not you?" he asked. For better or worse, donations are the lifeblood of every nonprofit, and the need to acquire new support every year can divert the leaders' energies away from the mission. Multiyear grants lend some stability for long-term growth.

Be sure the amount fits the need.

The first rule in grant making, as in medicine, is "Do no harm." Giving a group too much can, indeed, damage. "We've blown up some organizations with grants too large," admits Daryl Heald. He says that one must see where a little is enough. He has found two women in the Ukraine who take food to the children of Chernobyl with $100 a month. "It's enough to do what they do without overwhelming them," he says. Another foundation accustomed to making larger grants discovered that even the offer of $5,000 significantly skewed the interest of several churches considering a volunteer-based mentoring program. It led them to sign up for a project they were not prepared to continue when the grant ended.

Go narrow and deep.

Gaylord Swim of the GFC Foundation advocates resisting the temptation to give a little to many causes, but instead finding what is effective and giving significantly. He reminded a recent meeting of philanthropists, "It's better to invest deeply in one person who can change a city than to give $1 to 100,000 people." A growing number of donors are rethinking their strategy and choosing fewer programs and engaging them more deeply with funding and expertise.

Look for leaders, not programs.

Rick Wiederhold of the Elizabeth Brinn Foundation stresses that it is more important to find the right people than to discover the right program design. In funding more inner-city groups, he has realized that finding the most promising people and establishing a relationship of trust with them requires time and dedication. But once done, its value far outweighs its price, for those leaders have futures. "We fund chefs, not restaurants," he says. While some philanthropists categorically avoid "charismatic leaders," Wiederhold is bucking the trend and embracing investment in them because he believes that in this kind of work, the person and the program are often one.

Check the leader's motivation.

Bob Woodson says he only invests in leaders whose work predates funding and who would continue the program even if funding disappeared. That is the decisive test for people driven by faith commitment. If the potential of getting a grant is all that drives them, seek another partner. But if the person first ran the ministry out of the trunk of his or her car or apartment before getting paid, the commitment and motivation are probably authentic.

Find a sherpa.

An experienced guide who knows the territory can facilitate an expedition into unfamiliar terrain. A philanthropic advisor who specializes in faith-based organizations can provide good companionship for the journey. Peter Forbes says, "I wouldn't have known where to find the organizations myself. But having someone sort through them to find good people to invest in was invaluable." Pastors and people who have served on church mission committees also bring knowledge and expertise. Intermediaries who work in the area have a wealth of knowledge. Missions groups on the ground internationally are good resources.

Be willing to stretch.

Stepping outside the confines of one's own faith experience challenges anyone. When an evangelical Protestant visits a program with an interfaith chapel that has an altar, a cross, and a menorah, he may reject the whole program as having "confused theology." The first time an Episcopalian goes to a program including Pentecostal worship and people with their hands up in the air, it may feel uncomfortable. When a Roman Catholic encounters a street worker who does "Two-Minute Evangelism" promising instant eternal salvation, the theological clash prompts skepticism. These differences are much harder to bridge in practice than in theory. But it may be worth getting past the discomfort to cross the chasm and discover the gems on the other side.

Go and see.

Do not miss the experience of immersion in the world of the faith-based group you are funding, particularly if it is in an urban environment. Nothing can replace going into an unfamiliar neighborhood, even in a familiar city. The wife of a donor in Houston took the "plunge tour," driving with the group's leader past drug dealers, crack houses, and bullet-pocked apartments. After she hugged the kids in the program and walked through the tumbledown house where they lived, she understood. When she and her husband drove to the inner city the next Christmas Eve to personally deliver a check to the leader to buy a property for a new ministry home, a joy enveloped them that could only come from being there.

Conclusion
Motivation Matters

At a recent meeting of the Philanthropy Roundtable, Amy Kass, an award-winning professor who has taught literature and philosophy for a quarter of a century, challenged donors to contemplate another side of philanthropy. "Much is driven by accountability and the quest for results," she said. "But we lose sight of what it can do for the soul of the giver." As part of a project for civic reflection, she has compiled *The Perfect Gift*, a provocative collection of poetry and prose reflecting the philanthropic imagination.

A lively discussion ensued at a Philanthropy Roundtable session when Kass challenged the participating donors to read the reflections of Moses Maimonides, a Spanish-born philosopher and twelfth-century rabbi. In "The Book of Seeds," Maimonides writes about eight levels of *tzedakah*, a concept often translated as "charity," but which contains within it the sense of "righteousness" as well. The eight levels of *tzedakah* illustrate the degrees of relationship between a giver's heart and the receiver.

> There are eight levels of *tzedakah*, one better than the next. A high level, of which none is higher, is where one takes the hand of an Israelite and gives him a gift or loan, or makes a partnership with him, or finds him employment, in order to strengthen him until he needs to ask help of no one. *Concerning this it says, "And you will give strength to the resident alien, so he may live among you," as if to say, strengthen him until he will not falter or need.*

> Below this is one who gives *tzedakah* to the poor, not knowing to whom he gives, while the poor person does not know from whom he takes. *For this is [fulfillment of a] commandment for its own sake. . . .*

> Below this, the giver knows to whom he gives, and the poor person does not know from whom he takes. *For example: the rabbinic sages who went in secret, tossing coins in the door openings of the poor. In this case, it is proper and good if the alms officers do not behave precisely.*

> Below this, the poor person knows from whom he takes, and the giver does not know: *as per example of the greatest of the sages who would bundle small change in their sheets, and throw them over their shoulders, in sight of the poor, who took, so they would have no shame.*

Below this, one puts into another's hand before [the latter] asks.

Below this, one gives another after [the latter] asks.

Below this, one gives another less than is appropriate, in a pleasant manner.

Below this, one gives sorrowfully.[38]

An understanding emerged from the discussion that the better a man gives, the better he is. The highest level of giving encompasses a personal relationship, empowerment of another individual, trust between the donor and recipient, and a human touch between them. Its outcome is a changed life through a process that involves both parties. It maintains the dignity of the recipient, who is lifted to his feet by an extended hand and is empowered to stand alone. This kind of giving makes mutual transformation possible, even redemptive. Because faith-based groups most often work face-to-face with the people they serve, this element of mutuality is integral to involvement with them.

 The highest level of giving encompasses a personal relationship, empowerment of another individual, trust, and a human touch.

Jay Bennett, who heads the Kingdom Oil foundation in the Twin Cities, says, "The long historic money message is 'you need me, but I do not need you.' This is a fallacy. We need to move ministries and private capital into integrated relationship, based on covenant, brotherhood, and mutual submission of giftedness." He takes this aspect of giving seriously and personally. Bennett has entered into a partnership with Richard Coleman, an African American pastor who runs the foundation with him, and their rich relationship transcends the differences of their urban and suburban backgrounds. Bennett insists, "The financially bankrupt and the spiritually bankrupt bless one another in reciprocity before God."

 "The financially bankrupt and the spiritually bankrupt bless one another in reciprocity before God."

The effect may come as a surprise. Rick Wiederhold, who heads the Elizabeth Brinn Foundation in Wisconsin, was not looking for faith-based groups. He was willing to help them, but says he "didn't know how." After Bob Woodson came to Milwaukee and introduced him to some of the local faith-based leaders and what they were doing, Wiederhold says, "I got energized." As a businessman and a philanthropist, Wiederhold was looking for opportunities to invest wisely in his community. He discovered that local leaders like Cordelia Taylor were not only getting results, but that they had something to give him. He began to sense Cordelia's calling, which gives her power. As he put his energies behind the agenda she and her coworkers set for Family House, he was moved not only by their results, but by the kind of people

they are. "I envy them," he says. "They have this peace, they're so un-conflicted." In
reflecting on what Cordelia has given him, Wiederhold says, "My faith is stronger
now. I keep going back to get my battery recharged."

The Motive of *Agape*

The motives for giving are many. A recent survey of donors indicates that most
philanthropy in America springs from a desire to support worthwhile causes, a sense
of responsibility to share good fortune, and a desire to meet the community's critical
needs.[39] Each of these flows from good will toward others. The Greek word *agape*
encompasses this attitude. It embodies an unconditional commitment toward others
to lift them up and strengthen them. The highest form of love, *agape,* is unselfish and
altruistic—love for its own sake.

Different faiths acknowledge a surprisingly consistent wellspring of *agape* and
share an understanding of transcendent good. Ambassador James A. Joseph, who
served as the president of the Council on Foundations for fourteen years, writes,
"Those who study the relationship between faith and philanthropy are more likely to
point to the Semitic religions—Islam, Judaism, and Christianity—for their emphasis
on charity as a moral imperative, but echoes of a religious injunction can be found
elsewhere. Confucius saw benevolence as worth more than 'water or fire.' The scriptures of Theravada Buddhism describe charity as a way in which 'man and woman
alike can store up a well-hidden treasure.' "[40] Joseph points out that

> [T]he American model of the Christian gentleman providing charitable relief as part of
> his moral duty has its counterpart in the Parsi, who collected alms for the *punchayet* to
> distribute to the needy in Parsi communities; the Moslem who believed that *zakat*, con-
> tributing to the needs of deserving persons, was one of the five obligatory virtues of Islam;
> and the Jew whose moral tradition is dominated by the concept of *tzedakah*, the notion
> that charity is an obligation.[41]

All of these point to an understanding of natural law that transcends the partic-
ularities of time and place to appear in many civilizations. C. S. Lewis illustrates the
Tao, or the Way, in his book *The Abolition of Man*. This is no syncretistic approach to
religion, but instead is a sweeping demonstration of the breadth and permanence of
moral truth, which is so evident that all civilizations have grasped it, however imper-
fectly. Lewis compiles dozens of citations from the great religions of the world
throughout history and finds a remarkable similarity in the way they see compassion
as virtue.[42] Each of the world's great religions honors the concept of *agape* in a surprisingly consistent way. Both the Old Testament and the New Testament admonish
all people to "love your neighbor as yourself." Ancient Egyptians extolled the virtue
of giving "bread to the hungry, water to the thirsty, clothes to the naked and a
ferry boat to the boatless."[43] This echoes the New Testament admonition to feed the

hungry and clothe the naked.[44] The Old Testament proverb warns, "Those who oppress the poor insult their maker; but those who help the poor honor Him."[45] Caring for one's neighbor in a charitable way signals morality. The Buddhist proverb says: "Whatever happiness is in the world has arisen from a wish for the welfare of others; whatever misery there is has arisen from indulging selfishness."[46] The Qur'an urges the faithful to come to the aid of those in need, looking beyond the obvious: "True charity remembers not only those in need who ask, but also those who are prevented by some reason from asking."[47] Hebrew Scripture urges leaving a sheaf for the widow, the stranger, and the fatherless.[48] All of the world's religions have grasped one great transcendent truth: the human heart fulfills its highest capacity if it manifests *agape*, genuine unconditional love, toward other human beings.

An Investment in the Eternal

 The transforming power of love is at the heart of faith-based work. It is a dynamic, potent force. An investment here is an investment in the eternal.

The transforming power of love is at the heart of faith-based work. To the extent that people of faith embody *agape* and give it away, they handle a dynamic, potent force. If they genuinely seek to love selflessly, unconditionally, they will pour balm on wounded human souls. The transformative power of all faith grows from this one life-giving force. Whether the vehicle is a mentor in a school, a volunteer in an AIDS hospice, or a visitor to a prisoner, the love brought by these people makes their interaction meaningful, even if the love is unvoiced. Mother Teresa said, "There are no great deeds, only small deeds done with great love." Those who embody *agape* convey a spark of the divine beyond.

A gift to those who convey this spark of the transcendent is an investment in the eternal. And it brings joy.

Notes

1. "Faith and Philanthropy Report Shows Donors to Religion Are also Most Generous to Other Causes," news release, Independent Sector, June 27, 2002; Independent Sector and the National Council of Churches were reporting on a study by Atlantic Philanthropies, the Ford Foundation, and the Lilly Endowment.

2. See www.census.gov/prod/2003pubs/02statab/socinsur.

3. Ram Cnaan, *The Invisible Caring Hand: American Congregations and the Provision of Welfare* (New York: New York University Press, 2002), 9, 62. See also www.independentsector.org/media/InBriefPR.

4. See www.pewtrusts.com/pdf/rel_strategy_social_welfare.

5. Bryon Johnson, "Objective Hope: Assessing the Effectiveness of Faith-based Organizations: A Review of the Literature," Center for Research on Religion and Urban Civil Society, 2002, 7.

6. Calvin Edwards, "Evaluating Organizations," *The Edwards Report*, 2003.

7. Ibid.

8. Peter F. Drucker, *The Drucker Foundation Self-Assessment Tool*, foreword by Frances Hesselbein, (San Francisco: Jossey-Bass, 1999).

9. Byron Johnson, "A Better Kind of High: How Religious Commitment Reduces Drug Use among Poor Urban Teens," Center for Research on Religion and Urban Civil Society, 2002.

10. Johnson, "Objective Hope," 7.

11. Johnson, "A Better Kind of High."

12. John J. DiIulio Jr., in the introduction to Johnson's "Objective Hope," 6.

13. Catherine B. Hess, "Teen Challenge Training Center: Research Summation," 1975; "An Evaluation of the Teen Challenge Treatment Program," *Services Research Report*, National Institute on Drug Abuse, U.S. Department of Health, Education and Welfare (Washington, D.C., 1976).

14. Roger D. Thompson, "Teen Challenge of Chattanooga, TN: Survey of Alumni," 1994. Dr. Thompson, associate professor and head of the state Criminal Justice Department, conducted the independent survey in conjunction with the University of Tennessee at Chattanooga; and Aaron Todd Bicknese, "The Teen Challenge Drug Treatment Program in Comparative Perspective" (Ph.D. diss., Northwestern University, Evanston, IL, June 1999).

15. Byron R. Johnson with David B. Larson, *InnerChange Freedom Initiative: A Preliminary Evaluation of a Faith-Based Prison Program* (Philadelphia: University of Pennsylvania Center for Research on Religion and Urban Civil Society, 2003).

16. Scott Vander Stoep and Laurie Van Ark, "Evaluation of the Mentoring Program Kids Hope USA," Carl Frost Center for Social Science Research (Holland, MI: Hope College, 2003).

17. Melissa A. Barker and Greg Owen, "Urban Youth Initiative, Inc.: A Support Organization of the Memphis Leadership Foundation," Wilder Research Center, Amherst H. Wilder Foundation, March 2002.

18. Doug Easterling, "The Dark Side of Outcome Evaluation," *Grantmaker's Evaluation Network* 9, no. 1 (Winter 2001).

19. See Patrick Fagan, Claudia Horn, and Calvin W. Edwards, "The Promise of Outcome-Based Evaluation for Faith-Based Organizations," *Backgrounder,* Heritage Foundation, 2004.

20. Ibid, 4.

21. Ibid, 8.

22. Ibid.

23. William Schambra, "The Evaluation Wars," *Philanthropy*, May 2003.

24. Ibid.

25. Tom McCallie, interview with author. For a fuller explanation of these principles, see Pat McMillan, *Strategic Giving*, version 2/99 (Team Resources, 1994).

26. Barbara J. Elliott, "Equipping the Street Saints," *Philanthropy*, September 2002. This chapter is an expansion of the article.

27. Christine W. Letts, William Ryan, and Allen Grossman, "Virtuous Capital: What Foundations Can Learn from Venture Capitalists," *Harvard Business Review*, March–April 1997.

28. Ibid., 37.

29. Ibid., 41–43.

30. Michael E. Porter and Mark R. Kramer, "Philanthropy's New Agenda: Creating Value," *Harvard Business Review*, November–December 1999.

31. Stephen G. Greene, "Getting the Basics Right: Grant Makers Seek Effective Ways to Improve Charities' Operations," *Chronicle of Philanthropy*, May 3, 2001.

32. Ibid.

33. Ibid.

34. Michael E. Porter and Mark R. Kramer, "The Competitive Advantage of Corporate Philanthropy," *Harvard Business Review*, December 2002, 58–59.

35. Ibid.

36. Leadership Foundations of America is one of the largest networks of faith-based intermediaries. See www. LFofA.org.

37. See Amy Sherman's study on intermediaries, "Empowering Compassion," published by the Hudson Institute, 2002.

38. Moses Maimonides, quoted in *The Perfect Gift: The Philanthropic Imagination in Poetry and Prose*, ed. Amy Kass (Bloomington: Indiana University Press, 2002), 126. The selection is from *Hilchot Matanot Ani'im [Laws Concerning Gifts to the Poor]*, which appears in a tractate called *Sefer Zera'im [Book of Seeds]*, which is part of the *Mishneh Torah [Retelling of the Torah]*.

39. Seventy-nine percent, 69 percent, and 63 percent respectively (U.S. Trust Company, 2003).

40. James A. Joseph, "Building a Foundation for Faith and Family Philanthropy," in *Faith and Family Philanthropy: Grace, Gratitude, and Generosity*, ed. Joseph Foote (Washington, D.C.: National Center for Family Philanthropy, 2002).

41. Ibid.

42. C. S. Lewis, *The Abolition of Man* (New York: Macmillan, 1955), 95–121.

43. Ibid.

44. Matthew 25: 35–36.

45. Proverbs 14:31.

46. Quoted in Sir John Templeton, *Agape Love: A Tradition Found in Eight World Religions* (Philadelphia: Templeton Foundation Press, 1999), 60.

47. Sura 51:19.

48. Deuteromony 24:19.

Appendix

Donors' Toolbox for Evaluating
Faith-Based Organizations
The Legacy Group, Inc.

Tool 1. Donor's Giving Interest Inventory*
John L. Stanley

John L. Stanley is founder and president of the philanthropic advisory firm The Legacy Group, Inc. John has been helping donors navigate the world of philanthropy for thirty years.

Giving Interest Inventory

Step 1. What Causes Are Closest to Your Heart and Speak Directly to Your Convictions, Goals, and Calling?

Through our faith and personal experience, most of us have specific charitable causes to which we can relate. Check two general areas that you feel particularly strongly about helping:

____College/university scholarships

____World hunger

____Education

____Health

____Parenting

____Children and youth issues

____Young adults

____The arts

____Economic development

____International missions

____Domestic rural concerns

____Older adult (65+) issues

____Marriage and family

____Scientific research

____Entrepreneurship

____Domestic violence

____Women's issues

____Men's issues

____Community service/volunteerism

____The environment

____Inner city

____Evangelization/discipleship

____International disaster relief

____Seminary scholarships

____Other (identify below)

_____

*Copyright © 2004 by The Legacy Group, Inc.

Step 2. Whom or What Do You Want to Help?

Read through the lists and check two groups related to the charitable causes you selected in Step 1 that you have a strong concern for and would like to support with your charitable giving:

____Infants and preschool children (ages birth–3)	____Teachers
____Children (ages 3–13)	____Physically challenged
____High school students (ages 14–18)	____Mentally challenged
____College students	____Single mothers or fathers
____Seniors (ages 65 +)	____Clergy
____The homeless	____People in other countries
____New/first-time parents	____Women
____Minorities	____Chemical/substance abusers
____Hospitals/clinics	____Wildlife
____Men	____Artists
____Amateur athletes	____At-risk youth
____Musicians	____Immigrants/refugees
____Military personnel	____Other (identify below)
	_____

Step 3. What Individual, Community, or World Challenges Do You Wish to Address?

Your selected groups in Step 2 will have specific charitable needs. Check two situations that you would like your charitable giving to address:

____Physical or emotional pain	____Program enrichment
____Mentoring/role modeling	____Economic opportunities
____Habitat preservation	____Isolation
____Life transition	____Physical/emotional abuse
____Food and shelter	____Rebuilding one's life
____Improving education	____Strengthening personal faith
____Special skills or job training	____Illiteracy
____Life skills training	____Encouragement and motivation
____Financial challenges	____Overcoming illness and disease
____Fighting pollution	____Other (identify below)
	_____

Step 4. You and Your Partner—The Nonprofit Organization

Most charitable work is carried out by a specific type of nonprofit organization or ministry. From the list below, check one that you envision yourself partnering with:

____ Church or synagogue

____ General nonprofit enterprise

____ Community Development Association

____ Hospital or medical facility

____ Educational institution

____ Faith-based organization

____ Other (identify below)

_____

Step 5. Organizational Nature

Like businesses, charitable organizations come in many different descriptions and sizes as well as stages of maturity. Check the nature of the organization you envision helping:

____ Large and established

____ Small and established

____ Established but in decline, needs assistance for turnaround

____ Innovative and grassroots

____ Visionary organization in startup or growth phase

Step 6. Area of Service

What realm of influence should your charitable focus have? Check ONE.

____ International ____ National ____ Regional ____ Statewide ____ Local
____ Other (please identify) _____

Step 7. Creating your Personal Giving Mission

Use your choices for Step 1 to Step 6 to fill in the blanks below:

I feel strongly about helping causes related to _____ and _____,
(What Causes? . . . items checked in Step 1)

that specifically addresses the needs of _____ and _____ ,
(Whom or What Need?. . . items checked in Step 2)

who need help with _____ and _____.
(What Individual, Community, or World Challenges? . . . items checked in Step 3)

I envision fulfilling my charitable goals with a/an _____
(Organizational Partner . . . item checked in Step 4)

that is _____
(Organizational Nature . . . item checked in Step 5)

whose area of influence is _____ .
(Area of Service . . . item checked in step 6)

Tool 2. The Giving Continuum:
Defining Your Approach to Giving*

Place a dot on each line to indicate how your giving decisions are made. See what the pattern reveals to you.

Clear, almost single-minded intent · · · · · · Wide giving interests

Driven by passion for a cause · · · · · · Rational and disciplined towards giving

Actively looking for the outcome · · · · · · Responsive to the most recent requests

Keeping the end in mind—looking for great things to happen · · · · · · Satisfying many needs and maintaining minimum giving levels to protect the assets

Focused on the results of the gifts · · · · · · The process of giving is everything

Give it all away in one lifetime (with sunset provisions in case of death) · · · · · · Give in perpetuity, for all generations to come

Invest for the organization's long-term leadership success · · · · · · Invest for limited cycle of program-related gifts

Invest in the right leaders who cast a grand vision · · · · · · Review often and insist on accountability

The nonprofit leader is the expert · · · · · · The donor is the expert

Focus on strengths and invest in those with potential · · · · · · Focus on the most needy

Effectiveness · · · · · · Efficiency

A risk taker, investing heavily in a narrow area · · · · · · Lower risk, diversifying giving

Individualistic—responding to a calling to give · · · · · · Conforming to what others who care as I do are investing in

*Adapted with permission from Bob Buford's Giving Continuum. Copyright © 2004 by The Legacy Group, Inc.

Often, donors discover great satisfaction and impact if scores tend toward the left side of the continuum. What characterizes these donors?

1. They have internalized the conviction that it is a calling to give; it is entrepreneurial.

2. They give now rather than save for later.

3. They choose the right nonprofit leader, not just the right organization.

4. They build inch-wide, mile-deep relationships with charity leaders.

5. They measure results rather than where the dollars went.

6. They consider making contributions that build organizational capacity.

7. They encourage and empower the best leaders to exchange ideas.

8. They collaborate with other donors who give as they do.

Tool 3. What to Look for in a Philanthropic Advisor*
Peter A. Giersch

Peter Giersch is a senior advisor for The Legacy Group. Before joining The Legacy Group, he was a chapter director for Legatus International. A former National Endowment for Humanities scholar, he has written for local and national publications and has presented workshops on topics as diverse as monastic spirituality and communications technology.

A question has gained some popularity in philanthropic circles lately: "You worked hard at making your money, shouldn't you do the same when giving it away?" As with many of the things we purchase, acquire, or collect in life, we get so engrossed in the acquisition that we never think about what it will take to divest ourselves of the item. But selling a home, a car, a boat—even giving these things away—can prove more stressful and demanding than acquiring them.

To some, giving money away seems like the easiest occupation in the world. They bristle at the notion that one would need to hire an advisor for something that seems so easy. These people are mistaken in equating philanthropy with "giving money away." The confusion is understandable. The act of endowing a foundation, a charitable remainder trust, or some other philanthropic instrument is as simple as writing a check, and that might rightly be called giving money away. But as soon as one commits to distributing that money in service of a mission, cause, or purpose, philanthropy begins.

If donors fail to perceive the qualitative difference between writing checks and fulfilling a charitable mission, they will rarely, if ever, take the important step of seeking professional philanthropic advice. Most people feel that their lawyer, banker, or family financial planner can execute their philanthropic goals as a supplement to their current services. Again, this notion, though mistaken, is understandable because executing a philanthropic vision requires some key skills that can be performed by most financial advisors.

☑ Check writing
☑ Tax code compliance
☑ Maximizing deductions

*For more information on choosing a Philanthropic Advisor, contact The Legacy Group at www.philanthropyatwork.com. Copyright © 2004 by The Legacy Group, Inc.

☑ Leveraging PR benefits
☑ Reporting back to the client

If philanthropy involved strictly a transaction between donor and grantee, it would consist in no more than these activities. But the word *philanthropy* comes from two Greek words, which, when put together, mean "love of humanity." To be a philanthropist is to be a lover of humanity. One cannot discharge this sublime vocation simply by writing checks and maximizing deductions.

Philanthropy entails intentionality. It relies on discovering the deepest passions that motivate a donor and articulating a plan to direct resources toward realizing a vision. It demands striving toward results that aim high, but produce tangible outcomes. It encompasses the deepest motivation and the highest aspirations. And if done well, it brings joy.

Therefore, any donor with a passion to change the world can benefit from the help of an advisor who is dedicated to fulfilling the philanthropic interests of donors. Do such people exist? Certainly. It may be a cottage industry, but the Philanthropic Advisory Services Industry is beginning to take its work very seriously. As recently as the spring of 2004, a group of more than twenty philanthropic advisors met with noted ethicist Rush Kidder in New York to discuss creating industry standards in the areas of ethics and best practices.

Once the industry has matured and credentials can be better established for a philanthropic advisor, choosing one will be easy. But in the meantime, you can look for some important things when shopping for someone to help staff your foundation or advise your charitable giving.

First, a good philanthropic advisor must have the basics down cold. The five skills mentioned above, from check writing to reporting, are the foundation of good philanthropy. Your philanthropic advisor should know them well. There is perhaps one exception in the list, and that is maximizing tax deductions—a task usually best left to your accountant. But the rest are for your philanthropic advisor. These must be done flawlessly and with great consistency to allow philanthropy to express its real genius in the execution of mission.

Beyond these basic fiduciary skills, a wide worldview and broad experience mark great philanthropic advisors. One way to express this might be the phrase *crossover ability*. The best philanthropic advisors have the unique ability to walk with ease, charity, and mutual respect in any company, great or small. This trait demands priority because, on any given day, a philanthropic advisor might be required to go from a breakfast meeting with donors inside the Loop to a site visit by lunchtime at Cabrini Green with two Asian nuns who run a homeless shelter.

Far beyond being able to dress for any occasion and knowing how to speak each language, crossover ability entails truly understanding each world and knowing how to bridge the two. The world of donors and the world of nonprofits differ significantly, and many a grantor-grantee relationship has collapsed because of miscommunication, unrealistic expectations, or even willful misrepresentation—on either side of the table. Many greatly underestimate the cost in time, effort, and real dollars of these failed grants and relationships, and often ignore it when deciding how much to spend on foundation management.

If philanthropy separates itself from mere check writing by its emphasis on fulfilling a mission, then every philanthropic advisor should be an expert at the three key areas related to helping a mission-oriented group achieve its goals. These skills are:

☑ Achieving mission clarity
☑ Uniting a team around that mission
☑ Evaluating, correcting, and perfecting the mission

Harmony among the board of directors—especially when it is a family board—consistently predicts how focused and effective a foundation will be in distributing its dollars. An outside advisor can promote order and professionalism with objectivity while acting as a shock absorber for the most contentious issues. As a third party, the advisor can also help prevent mission drift and power struggles that often hamper effective foundations.

Finally, one additional skill to look for in a philanthropic advisor is the ability to work independently. Most donors live in a world that is extremely mobile, far reaching, and full of opportunities. They need from their advisors consistent performance despite the donor's variable commitment. In the inevitable absence of the donor or key decision maker, a good philanthropic advisor must be able to execute donor intent without hesitation or doubt—and must be empowered to do so by the donor.

Philanthropy is a grand and noble undertaking, a serious commitment which should not be taken lightly. By engaging a philanthropic advisor, the donor is respecting the tremendous potential and importance of the charitable inclination. Moreover, when donors choose their philanthropic advisor carefully and well they are ensuring that their vision of a new and better world will be transformed into the reality of changed lives.

Tool 4. Tax and Legal Ramifications of Giving to Faith-Based Organizations*
Patricia G. Woehrer

Pat Woehrer directs the operations of two private foundations, Vine and Branches Foundation and Foundation of Faith, as senior philanthropic advisor for The Legacy Group. Eleven years at The Bradley Foundation in Milwaukee, Wisconsin, equipped her with a wide range of knowledge and a wealth of experience in navigating the startup of a private foundation, fulfillment of the donor's values and vision, and foundation compliance and tax issues.

Giving Vehicles

- A *private foundation* is an independent charitable trust or corporation that makes contributions to many charitable organizations. It allows you to maintain maximum operational control and is often set up as a family foundation to give a family purpose and a means to work together. While it allows you to retain the most control, it is subject to more IRS regulations and has the least favorable tax benefits of the following choices.

- A *supporting organization* is a charitable trust or corporation tied to specific charities. If you are interested in creating a close relationship with specific charities and are willing to give up majority representation on the board for a superior tax benefit, this vehicle is worth considering.

- A *donor-advised fund* is a gifting account commingled with other accounts governed by a sponsoring entity, often a community foundation. Donor-advised funds do not require the time and administrative expense of a private foundation or a supporting organization. The donor realizes the tax deduction the year the gift is made to the fund, even if it is not distributed in contributions until later. The drawback of donor-advised funds is in the

*Copyright © 2004 by The Legacy Group, Inc.

amount of control retained. The donor may only recommend contributions from this fund to qualified charities; the governing board may or may not ratify those choices.

- *Pooled funds*, such as community foundations or the United Way, are publicly supported entities that sustain a large number of charities in the broader community and offer the same tax benefit as a direct gift to a charity. Unless the entity offers a designation opportunity, funds are allocated by that entity at their discretion. Designated gifts may or may not be charged a processing fee to help sustain the pooled fund's operations.

- *Planned giving vehicles*, such as charitable remainder trusts, allow the donor to make a contribution to a single charity, and receive all or a portion of the earnings from the trust for an agreed upon time period. The tax deduction is realized by the donor at the time the initial gift is made, and the ownership of the funds is transferred to the charity at that time. The principal may then be used by the charity after the agreed upon time period has concluded.

- *Non-cash gifts*, such as stock or property, present yet another method of contributing to charitable organizations and should be considered in conjunction with an overall philanthropic plan with an appropriate advisor.

In addition to tax benefits and control, other factors to consider in choosing an appropriate giving vehicle include the amount of money targeted for donation and any desire for anonymity. In addition, tax benefits should always be considered with a tax advisor in the broader context of the donor's overall financial position.

Deductibility of Contributions to Churches

Historically, many private foundations chose to avoid funding churches or other specifically religious organizations as a matter of course. Yet, the Internal Revenue Service identifies religious purpose as one of six types of charitable organizations: religious, charitable, scientific, literary, educational, or for the prevention of cruelty to children and animals. The IRS does not require churches to apply for a 501(c)(3) status, for their very nature is deemed as inherently public activity. However, IRS utilizes a 14-point attribute test to identify a church. Of those, the most critical is whether the organization has, first, a regular body of congregants who, second, regularly assemble for worship. Churches may, and are encouraged to, apply for 501(c)(3) publicly supported charitable status if they provide substantial human service programs in addition to regular church activity.

A private foundation giving to a church without a 501(c)(3) should document the church's existence as an entity by requesting a minimum of two documents demonstrating the IRS guidelines, such as its bylaws and list of board members, and the self-reported number of congregants. Churches receiving government support are required to set up separate bank accounts from the church for those funds, perform regular financial reporting to the grantor, and normally design their program to separate the spiritual component, in the event a program constituent wishes to participate only in the secular portion of the human service provided.

Supporting a Church Program vs. Separate Faith-Based Organization

For efficiency, many churches provide social services under the church structure (and charitable status) and financial support of its members until the program is well established. An event usually triggers a change to protect both the church and the social program financially as the latter grows in budget, scope, and risk. This important change highlights the legal differences in organizational rules for hiring, religious program content, main-tenance of public support status, and fund reporting. When considering funding to either entity, consider the program's source of control (responsible board of directors) and capacity to manage its growth. As a donor, ask yourself "what if" scenario questions.

Advanced Ruling Period

Examine the IRS tax-exempt determination letter of a charitable organization for an "advanced ruling period." The IRS uses this date, usually five years from the date the organization began its activity, as a crucial initial period to test the organization's ability to become "publicly supported" by a broad variety of sources. Upon good due diligence, a donor may make a contribution within ninety days of expiration of the advanced ruling date, assuming the organization has filed for and is awaiting its permanent status. Even among sophisticated nonprofit organizations, the expired letter may inadvertently be used in a funding application.

Pass-Through Gifts

Private foundations cannot designate a gift to a specific person or entity, through another organization, to whom they could not otherwise give directly. For example, if a foundation desires to support a particular missionary, the foundation may not provide a contribution to a church and require the church to re-gift it to a named missionary or an entity not recognized as exempt by the IRS. In other words, the foundation must release control of the funds to the first grantee in order to count it toward its minimum distribution requirement and also to avoid a penalty tax.

Gift Size

In a donor's haste to see a wonderful new idea get off the ground quickly, or to liberate an organization from laboring in fundraising, a gift too large can trigger IRS trouble for both parties. By shifting the organization's support formula from that of a broad base to a more singular base, IRS may reclassify the organization as a private foundation. You can avoid this by structuring a very large gift as an "unusual gift." A philanthropic or tax advisor can help with various components to such a gift.

Self-Dealing and Private Inurement

With any contribution, a private foundation donor should examine any potential for self-dealing when committing funds to a church or faith-based organization. In essence, a donor cannot privately benefit through certain financial transactions with the foundation. The rule extends to other individuals or entities associated with the foundation via family ties or substantial support to the foundation; see an attorney for a complete understanding of "disqualified persons." (Even if the foundation benefits in some way from the transaction, it may be deemed as *self-dealing*.)

Private inurement ranges widely, focused on specific business transactions that result in the flow of income or assets away from the foundation and toward a person related to the foundation. Among other transactions, particularly note *certain assumptions of liability*, such as fulfillment of personal donation pledges, private memberships/dues, and ticket purchases. Donors to private foundations cannot use the foundation assets to pay a personal pledge. Particularly in a church setting, it is common to receive pledge cards. Avoid completing such pledge commitments in the event you wish the foundation to make the gift according to its application procedures. Also, do not allow the foundation to accept tickets or invitations to events where the donor will benefit from dinner, performance, etc., without specific charitable activity. If desiring to attend, the donor should personally pay for the tickets.

Private benefit is a broad area that focuses on the operations of the foundation's tax-exempt purpose being organized for the benefit of specific individuals—related or not. The key: tax-exempt purposes are *public* purposes.

Funding International Agencies

Nearly every denomination in the United States maintains some form of charitable work in foreign countries, whether direct relief, health intervention, economic development, education, or evangelization. Internal Revenue code restricts both individuals and private foundations to supporting 501(c)(3) publicly supported charities. A contribution to a U.S. religious denomination for international work constitutes a gift to a U.S. charity for a foundation's tax purposes, but what if the organization has purely international roots and lacks IRS recognized charitable status? Individuals should consult IRS publication 526.

Foundations, however, may utilize three traditional methods to effectively give to international organizations: conduct expenditure accounting responsibility to demonstrate the funds were spent with charitable purposes, find a U.S. sponsoring organization, or produce an affidavit documenting the organization's purposes and practices as equivalent to the IRS charitable code. In recent years, new organizations have been created that can receive 501(c)(3) contributions from individuals or foundations for redistribution to foreign programs, such as the Virtual Foundation. Also, the Council on Foundations and affinity groups such as Grantmakers Without Borders provide international grant-making information to foundations.

Patriot Act

Quickly after the onset of terrorism on U.S. soil in September 2001, donors became responsible for adding to their due diligence research of their grantees the assurance that no potential exists of supporting terrorism directly or indirectly through grant support for the benefit of certain individuals or entities. The U.S.A. Patriot Act, enacted in October 2001, increases the government's access to information to help defend national security and increases the responsibility of corporations and donors to consider with whom they are associated. Donors can check four separate lists of names of organizations and individuals that are suspect or known to be engaged in some support of terrorism. In addition, those that the recipient organization associates with are also to be checked. Compliance services and software are available to assist. The U.S. International Grantmaking Project of the Council on Foundations offers links to additional information at www.usig.org.

Revocation of the Tax-Exempt Status

An organization maintains its nonprofit status by strictly adhering to the Internal Revenue code and regulations with a focus on charitable purpose and sources of financial support. The organization's leadership must be well versed in these matters. Should an organization's charitable status change to another sub-status or be revoked, the deductibility of contributions will change, affecting donors. And if a donor is responsible for the status change, a penalty tax may result to both parties.

Like other nonprofit organizations, churches face restrictions in lobbying and political campaign activities. The rules revolve around activities identified as partisan for or against particular candidates. Churches and 501(c)(3) organizations must not participate in political campaigns on behalf of or in opposition to any candidates for elective public office, either directly or indirectly. Contributions by such organizations to political campaign funds are prohibited. *Nonpartisan* voter education or registration drives may be conducted. A church may invite, with *equal opportunity*, candidates to speak to their congregations. Religious leaders may speak personally about political issues, but must be clear that they are not representing their church in that communication.

Tool 5. Analyzing Nonprofit Financial Statements*
Mary Kay Mark

Mary Kay Mark is the chief financial officer for The Legacy Group and a senior philanthropic advisor. She brings to the task experience as the administrator of a Milwaukee-based family foundation and has served several corporations in financial positions. She is a certified public accountant.

Although it requires effort, it is important in the due diligence process to understand a nonprofit's financial statements in order to determine the organization's stability. A donor should invest this time to glimpse other facets of a nonprofit that may not be apparent during site visits or in discussions with a faith-based leader.

Types of Financial Statements

Financial statements give information based on different time periods. To understand an organization's financial past, a donor should review the Income Statement, or in nonprofit terms, the Statement of Activities. This financial statement tells whether the organization's revenues adequately covered expenditures over a designated time period. Simply put, the amounts received need to cover the amounts disbursed. To understand a nonprofit's current financials, a donor should review the Balance Sheet, or Statement of Financial Position. This statement shows the assets, liabilities, and net assets of an organization. Assets consist of items owned, while liabilities are amounts owed. Net assets equal the difference between the total assets and the total liabilities. Finally, to understand an organization's financial future, reviewing budgets or cash flow projections can provide the necessary information to determine the solidity of a nonprofit's financial future.

The Audit Opinion

A good starting point in reviewing financial statements is an organization's audit opinion. Audited statements are completed by an independent third party, a financial expert, who verifies that the amounts shown on the financial statements are accurate and fair. Begin by examining the auditor's opinion to see that it is unqualified. The unqualified opinion includes a standard sentence that the financial statements present fairly, in all material aspects, the financial position of the organization. Under an unqualified opinion, you have reasonable assurance that you can rely upon the numbers. If any reference to an exception or to the organization's status as a continuing concern appears, you have uncovered a serious red flag.

An auditor's opinion may include other items of concern, such as any outstanding litigations, inadequate internal controls, or uncertainties pertaining to IRS or state audits. If the auditor is unable to render an opinion, ask some serious questions of the organization's leadership before contributing anything. Many smaller or religious organizations are not required to have an audit performed, and the absence of an audit is not necessarily a red flag. In these situations, you will want to ensure that the person preparing the statements

*Copyright © 2004 by The Legacy Group, Inc.

has financial training or qualifications necessary to prepare them reliably. References to the financial statements' notes, found at the end of audited statements, can clarify other notable financial information.

The Statement of Activities

After reviewing the opinion, address the Statement of Activities first. At least two, and preferably three, years of analyzed financial data should appear. Comparative data can show trends and patterns that one year of data will not provide. Begin with the overall results of the time periods presented, which are usually arranged in one-year segments. Review the bottom line of the Statement of Activities to see if the change in net assets is positive or negative. A positive change in net assets means that revenue exceeded expenses. Alternatively, a negative change in net assets indicates that expenses eclipsed revenue. A negative change for the past two years can signal financial trouble. This requires some explanation from the nonprofit's leadership.

Next, focus on support and revenue, present at the statement's top portion. Contributions and earned revenue, alone, compose nonprofit revenue. Look to see how much of the nonprofit's income is from donations and how much from earned income. Generally, a higher percentage of earned income creates self-sufficiency and financial stability. Unfortunately, earned revenue is more likely to be the exception rather than the norm, particularly in a faith-based nonprofit. In the area of support, how much originates with the government, and how much comes from private or foundation donations? Some experts feel a healthy faith-based group derives at least 80 percent of its revenue from individuals and the remainder from government and foundations. While some faith-based organizations do accept government funding for their programs, government grants can bear some significant drawbacks. The high cost of administering a government grant can ultimately reduce the grant's value. Significant funding from a single source should also ignite concern. Exercise great caution if one source provides 20 percent or more of total revenue. The loss of that one funding source could plunge an organization into critical financial straits. Once again, it is appropriate to ask questions of the nonprofit leaders.

Other flags on the Statement of Activities include excessive fund-raising, administrative, or payroll expenses, which could indicate wastefulness or a poorly run organization. On the other hand, it could merely indicate that the nonprofit leaders have improperly split out administrative costs and not allocated appropriate amounts to programs, resulting in program-related costs understated and administrative costs overstated. Emphasize the importance of statement preparation by a financially trained person. Ask questions about large amounts in the miscellaneous expense category. Understand that administrative costs of large national or international organizations will surpass those of small grassroots organizations. Finally, trends that indicate declining revenues, increasing operating losses, or elimination of programs can denote financial uncertainty.

The Statement of Financial Position

Next, review the Statement of Financial Position. Start again with an overall picture. Are the nonprofit's assets greater than its liabilities? If so, the net assets will be positive, a good start in confirming financial stability. Too many years of negative net assets will lead to an organization's demise. Compare cash—an asset—with current liabilities to confirm that the organization can pay its bills out of the cash it has on hand. If current liabilities exceed available cash, this could signal an unstable financial situation rooted in cash flow problems. Examine total assets on hand. Even if a nonprofit has substantial assets, if they consist entirely of inventory, buildings, or receivables, cash flow problems could escalate. None of those assets can pay the bills if cash is tight.

Next, examine the amount of accumulated depreciation on the fixed assets. If the accumulated depreciation on buildings and equipment approaches the total value of the assets, it could mean that assets are old and will need replacement in the near future. Does the organization have a plan and the funds available to replace worn out assets? Look at several years' endowment and reserves. If they erode over time, determine whether or not the endowment is funding operations, which is strictly prohibited.

Of course, the opposite situation could justify declining funding. If an organization has more than two years of operating expenses on hand in cash and investments, you should raise the question of financial need. Give the nonprofit a chance to explain large increases in endowments or investments that may be earmarked for significant projects in the future. If not, perhaps a less well-off organization could better utilize your funds.

Also review the liabilities section of the Statement of Financial Position. One line item needs particular scrutiny: payroll tax liability (found under the current liabilities section of a financial statement.) A large balance could indicate the nonprofit uses payroll taxes withheld from employees to pay for operations. The IRS will show little mercy before seizing any and all assets to satisfy a tax levy, regardless if the funds seized are grant payments just made by an unsuspecting donor. On the other hand, if payroll tax liability is not listed, inquire as to the balance. It is rare for an organization to have no payroll tax liabilities, so if a nonprofit insists that it has none, be wary. Continuing in the liabilities section, look for a line item entitled deferred revenue or refundable advance. This refers to funds received that relate to work not yet performed or to an uncompleted contract. If the nonprofit went out of business today, it would have to return those funds. Unless a corresponding amount of cash is on hand to cover the advances, the company is not making ends meet.

The Budget

Third, review the budget to gauge future financial health. A budget should exist for the nonprofit as a whole and for any projects for which an organization is seeking support. If the budget is for a project, the biggest question is whether or not the community will receive a benefit at least equal to the amount of your investment. Compare the total cost of the project to the amount that you are being asked to support. You should not be expected to support an entire project. If possible, compare the total cost of the project to similar projects of other organizations. The budget should include a solid plan for revenues and not just focus on the expense side of the equation. Expenses should seem reasonable when compared to sustainable income. Ideally, the income will include a mix of individual and foundation funding and both earned and contributed revenue, although faith-based organizations usually have little earned revenue.

With the added information gleaned from review of the financial statements, the financial health of a nonprofit should be easier to gauge. These statements convey a more complete picture of the nonprofit in question, rounding out the evaluation. A little thoughtful digging should give you reasonable assurance that the funds contributed will not go into a "black hole," but rather will make a lasting contribution to a community.

Tool 6. Faith-Based Organizations from A to Z: A Donor's Guide*
Barbara J. Elliott

Barbara Elliott is the founder of the Center for Renewal in Houston, Texas, a resource center for faith-based organizations working to renew America's cities. She is also a philanthropic advisor with the Legacy Group.

Peter Drucker has observed that the bottom line for nonprofits is changed human lives. The best of the faith-based organizations are innovative, cost-effective, results oriented, and they look for the bottom line. They direct their efforts to changing people from the inside out through complete transformation. The questions below help determine which organizations are worthy of support. Quite often, small, relatively unknown faith-based groups toiling on the streets of our cities work very effectively. Fostering growth here, at the grassroots level of the seedlings of civil society, will revitalize America's communities from within. Marvin Olasky and Robert Woodson have written wisely on these matters, and their thinking is reflected here.

Accountability: Does the organization demand accountability of the people it serves? Are the providers held accountable to standards of performance and financial responsibility?

Bonding: Does the program foster one-to-one relationships between those giving and those receiving? Is mentoring an important part of the relationship? The more relational the work, the more likely it will change lives.

Character: Does the organization build character in the recipients? Is there a moral component to what it offers? If it does not impart good character and virtue, lasting improvement is less likely.

Discernment: Do the providers use discerning judgment to give help on an individual basis that considers individual needs? Do they tailor solutions to fit each person?

Entrepreneurial: Does the group create entrepreneurial opportunities for people who want to become whole and self-supporting? Does it find innovative ways to create enterprises to help support its work with revenue streams?

Families: Does the organization focus on the family as the most important unit of social order and the key to renewing both individuals and communities? Dealing with children or adults in isolation cannot get to the root of most social disorders.

God: Do the providers treat each participant as a valuable creation of God and communicate his love? Meeting material needs without addressing spiritual needs is far too little.

Hand up not a Handout: Does the program offer a hand up to people in temporary need, empowering them to leave dependency, or does it merely provide a handout?

Integrity: Do the leaders and the individuals doing the work model integrity and inculcate it in those they serve?

Justice: Does this approach address the deepest issues that affect the social justice of people in need? Does it raise them up through systemic changes?

*Copyright © 2004 by Barbara J. Elliott

Knowledge: Is the work based on knowledge of the community's needs? Does the group know of other local service providers doing similar work? Are the leaders aware of best practices of other similar groups nationally?

Love: Mother Teresa said, "There are no great deeds, only small deeds done with great love." Do these people show love to those for whom they care?

Motivation: Why did the people behind the organization begin it? Why do the people working with them do it?

Neighborhood: Does this organization have roots in the neighborhood and the support of the neighbors? What is their reputation at the grassroots level? Are they part of a broader coalition of people committed to renewing the community from within?

Outcomes: Does the program have a success rate that can be quantified? Have outside studies validated its results? Do they implement Outcomes-Based Evaluation?

Participation: Does the program utilize capabilities of volunteers in the community? A CEO ladling soup is wasted talent in a nonprofit that needs a business plan. Creative thinking can harness the experience of auto mechanics, electricians, computer programmers, accountants, and anyone with a willing heart.

Questions: Do providers ask the recipients direct questions to determine need? Can the providers answer the donors' hard questions?

Reconciliation: Does this approach reconcile individuals across the divides of race, denomination, socioeconomic level, and political persuasion?

Skills: Does the organization help people master literacy and job skills? Does it impart life skills such as parenting or managing time and money?

Transformation: Does this approach aim beyond treating symptoms to accomplish transformation of the people served?

Understanding but Unswerving: Do the leaders have the strength of character to be understanding of failures, yet unswervingly enforce high standards? Setting the bar high—whether for educational or moral standards—produces better results.

Volunteers: Does the program effectively mobilize volunteer talent from the community, providing training, evaluation, and opportunity for reflection?

Work: Does the program teach the value of working reliably, following instructions, completing tasks, and exemplifying excellence in work?

X-tra Effort: Are the people running this program willing to walk the second mile with the people they serve? Are they committed to continuing the work, even if funding is tight?

You: Does this cause resonate with you? Does the organization fit your convictions, speak to your heart, and call you? Prayerfully consider whether this is where you can best contribute your time, talent, or treasure.

Zip Code: People living in the same zip code as those they serve effect the most change. They know the neighborhood, the people, and the local dynamics. Such people are more likely to be worthy of your support.

Tool 7. Checklist for a Site Visit*
Mary Kay Mark

Preparation for the Visit

- Review all available resources on the organization—Web site, brochures, annual report, financial statements

- Familiarize yourself with the faith-based sector in which the program exists, so you can put the organization in the proper context

- Talk to others who are knowledgeable in the field or about the organization

Setting up the Meeting

- Request sixty to seventy minutes of their time and honor it

- Tours should be minimal and only necessary for program information

- Meet with executive director, one staff person, and consider having a client there to provide *brief* testimony; board members welcome, sometimes required, depending on the proposal

- Confirm address and obtain driving directions and parking information

- Confirm meeting two to three days ahead with all parties involved

Introductions at the Meeting

- Create a genuine rapport and put the staff at ease as quickly as possible. Explain your mission and goals, followed by any questions they have about you. Note whether the applicant asks about your mission at all. If yes, it can signal an attitude of partnership.

Questions

Personal history of executive director:

- Where was he or she raised, how long has he or she lived in the area? Does he/she live in the zip code of his/her service area?

- What are his/her life's passions?

- Who has influenced or mentored him/her?

- What brought him or her to this position? When?

- Why does he or she do this kind of work? (Find out the motivation.)

Organizational/program information:

- Brief historical picture and current mission

- Type of board (active, working, policy)

- The programs—what do they do, and why? What works and what does not work?

- Does the organization have a strategic plan in place?

- What are the organization's strengths?

- How financially healthy is the organization (broad support, revenue, major changes)?

*Copyright © 2004 by The Legacy Group, Inc. All rights reserved.

- What type of leadership does the board practice?
- What kind of rapport does the executive director have with the board? Observe if at all possible.
- What strengths/skills do the board members contribute?
- What are the staff's qualifications, and what is the turnover rate?
- How has the organization changed in the last couple of years?
- What still needs to change?
- What will be the organization's greatest challenge/obstacle this year?
- If the executive director could change one thing, what would it be?
- What is the executive director's/organization's vision for five years in the future?
- Why is this project needed? What value will it bring to constituents?
- Is the value being brought to those most severely affected by the problem?
- Was it well researched and thought out? Test-marketed? Duplicative? Cost-effective?
- Did they work from a model? Will they share a model if they develop one?
- How do they measure success? When? What outcomes are expected and documented?
- How long do they maintain contact with constituents?
- If I do not fund them, what will happen to the program?
- If I do fund them, will they come back to me every year?

After the Site Visit

Evaluation:
- Overall, do my goals and mission match those of the applicant?
- Does the organization have a clear purpose?
- Is the plan feasible?
- Are they doing it the right way?
- Is the board balanced and capable?
- Does the leadership possess entrepreneurial characteristics and capacity to grow and innovate?
- Do they have appropriate staff?
- Do they have adequate support?
- Are the foundation dollars really needed?
- Are there other obvious needs at the organization perhaps more urgent than this request?
- Was there positive activity at the site visit?
- How do people at the site relate to one another?
- Is there pride in their work?
- Is the facility in good repair and appropriate to the organization's needs?
- Is this a risky grant for me? If so, how much would I be risking?
- Where is the organization its life cycle, and what impact does that have on the proposal?

Tool 8. Checklist for Due Diligence*
Patricia G. Woehrer

Major Gift Due Diligence

I. Organizational Information

A. Contact information:

Organization: _____

Address: _____

_____

Phone: _____

Fax: _____

Executive Director: _____

E-mail: _____

Web site: _____

Referred by: _____

B. Document collection:

☐ IRS letter of tax-exempt determination 501(c)(3) and public support status [i.e., 509(a)(1)], verified

☐ Annual operating budget (current year *and* prior year)

☐ Most recent informational tax return 990

☐ Annual report

☐ Organization mission statement

☐ Board of directors list

☐ Biographies of professional staff

☐ Sample brochures and/or print materials

☐ Most current financial audit and for two years prior

☐ Business plan

C. Organization analysis via documents, interviews, and site visit:

1. *Background information*

   The following questions are adapted from the Peter F. Drucker Foundation's Self-Assessment Tool.

   • What is their mission?

   • Whom do they serve?

   • What do they value?

   • How do they measure their program's success?

   • What is their organization's biggest challenge?

*Copyright © 2004 by The Legacy Group, Inc. All rights reserved.

2. Organizational Overview

- ☐ Total number of paid staff and volunteers
- ☐ Organization's brief history
- ☐ Description of the population served
- ☐ Major accomplishments
- ☐ Passion, commitment
- ☐ Vision for the future
- ☐ Staff cohesiveness (morale, professionalism, stability)
- ☐ Organizational capacity and competency
- ☐ Fiscal success
- ☐ Position in organizational life cycle
- ☐ What kind of public attention and media coverage has this work received? Awards?
- ☐ Who else is doing this work and how is this organization different from them?
- ☐ Was a site visit performed?
- ☐ Is the facility serving the organization well? Is it clean and in good repair, with adequate space?

3. Board of directors' qualifications and governance

- ☐ Experience/knowledge in the service area
- ☐ Business/management experience
- ☐ Number and diversity (financial, legal, consumer, human resources, management, marketing, program)
- ☐ Board style (policy, active, working)
- ☐ Standing committees (executive, finance, audit, fund-raising, personnel, program, other)
- ☐ Financial participation in organization
- ☐ Constituent representation
- ☐ Community visibility and influence
- ☐ Frequency of board meetings
- ☐ Effective use of strategic plan

4. Leadership and staff qualifications

- ☐ Leadership ability of executive director
- ☐ Experience/knowledge in the service area
- ☐ Business/management/nonprofit experience
- ☐ Community visibility and influence

Specific Questions for Assessing Leadership of Christ-centered Organizations

☐ What has the faith journey of the leader been?

☐ Does this leader demonstrate the fruits of the spirit—love, joy, peace, patience, humility, kindness, goodness, faithfulness, gentleness, and self-control?

☐ To whom is the leader spiritually accountable?

☐ Are the staff members followers of Christ? Are the volunteers?

☐ Is the goal of the organization rooted in a clear Kingdom vision?

☐ Is the work Holy Spirit-led, where God is already at work?

☐ In what way is the statement of faith integrated into its methods?

☐ If conversion and discipleship are clear goals of the program, is there structured follow-up to make the changes lasting?

☐ In what way is this work oriented to the two great commandments: love of God and love of one's neighbor?

☐ If the organization provides social services, is the use of commodities embedded in relationship to produce lasting spiritual transformation?

☐ Can the outcomes be expressed in terms of clearly changed human lives?

☐ To what extent is prayer a part of the organization's modus operandi?

☐ Is there a commitment to excellence in all things?

5. *Financial analysis:*

Sources of support for operations from the most recent audited statement:

Type of support	*Amount*	*Percent of total*
☐ Contributions from individuals		
☐ Foundations		
☐ Corporations		
☐ Churches		
☐ In-kind support		
☐ Endowment income		
☐ Program/client service fees		
☐ Earned income via business venture		
☐ Government grants/contracts		
☐ United Way/other federated campaign		
☐ Other revenue (specify)		
☐ What is the economic engine?		

Operating and program expenses:

Like investing, making charitable gifts carries certain levels of risk. How financially risky would this gift be?

☐ Operating expense budget:
Direct service _____ % Fund-raising _____ % Management _____%

☐ Operating reserves available: $_____
Number of months' expenses on hand: _____

☐ Operating surpluses or deficits for last three years:
Year 1 $_____   Year 2 $_____   Year 3 $_____

Reasons for surplus or deficit: _____
_____
_____

☐ Any current operational debt: $_____
Reason: _____
_____

☐ Any capital debt: $ _____
Reason: _____
_____

☐ Does the organization have any legal matters pending?
Yes_____   No_____
If yes, Reason: _____
_____
_____

☐ Is there certification of financial accountability? ECFA (Evangelical Council for Financial Accountability), BBB (Better Business Bureau), or other?
_____
_____

II. Program Information

A. Overview

☐ Current programs: goals, objectives
☐ History
☐ Quality of programs
☐ Demonstrated innovation
☐ Growth pattern
☐ Has this program ever been successfully replicated?

B. Validation of program outcomes (attach studies):

Demonstrated evidence of life transformation (beyond activities; i.e., changed behavior/attitudes)

☐ Outcomes-Based Evaluation, internal
☐ External evaluation by independent firm
☐ Cost/benefit ratio based on current services provided
☐ External sociological study by academic institution
☐ Research on comparable methodology and results
☐ Demonstrated evidence of life transformation (beyond activities; i.e., changed behavior/attitudes)

C. Proposal data:

☐ Project proposal, clearly stated

☐ Demonstrated need

☐ Expectations and measurements

☐ Complete budget specific to this project

☐ Amount requested: $_____

☐ Is multiyear support requested?   Yes _____   No _____

☐ Date/s grant payment/s needed by: _____

☐ Other sources of support for proposed project

☐ Viability of project/project's priority within organization

☐ Future/ongoing funding plan for project

☐ Project relationship to foundation mission

☐ Duration of project _____ (approximate dates)

D. Additional considerations for specific project types:

Building project:	complete funding plan; architectural renderings; estimated ground-breaking date; finishing, furnishing, and equipment; timeline for completion
Endowment:	use of funds, funding plan, need analysis, matching grant opportunities
Entrepreneurial venture:	solid business plan, advisory board, capacity of organization, marketability of product, competition, innovation, business experience/background of leadership, financial tools/resources/knowledge, exit strategy
Grassroots:	community support, community building efforts; capacity of fund-raising, board leadership, and program development (growth); resourcefulness, ongoing staff development
Media production:	marketing efforts, target and scope of audience, ownership of product, academic support and use, quality assurance, distribution strategy, royalties

III. Decision

☐ Does this project/program fit my values, personal mission, and goals?

☐ Is this the right organization to carry out the project?

☐ Under what circumstances would I say no?

☐ What would be an appropriate amount both for me, as a donor, and the organization?

☐ Should I consider leveraging my gift with a challenge or matching grant, or other strategic method?

☐ What type of recognition would be appropriate, if any?

☐ Is a grant agreement necessary to protect my gift?

☐ How will I monitor the organization's progress?

- Written report
- Follow-up site visit
- Volunteer on-site
- Become a board member

☐ Would I accept a future request?

Contact Information

Below is contact information for the groups mentioned in the text. For a fuller directory of faith-based organizations throughout the country, see www.streetsaints.com. Profiles of their work appear in the companion volume to this book, *Street Saints: Renewing America's Cities* (Templeton Foundation Press, 2004).

Aldine Y.O.U.T.H.: www.aldineyouth.org

American Institute of Philanthropy: www.charitywatch.org

Best Friends Foundation: www.bestfriendsfoundation.org

Better Business Bureau Wise Giving Guide Alliance: www.give.org

Boys & Girls Clubs of America: www.bgca.org

Boy Scouts of America: www.scouting.org

Lynde and Harry Bradley Foundation: www.bradleyfdn.org

Bridges to Life: www.bridgestolife.org

Brookwood Community: www.brookwoodcommunity.org

Calvin Edwards & Company: www.calvinedwardscompany.com

Carver Academy: www.thecarveracademy.com

Center for Effective Philanthropy: www.effectivephilanthropy.com

Center for Renewal: www.centerforrenewal.org

The Center on Philanthropy at Indiana University: www.philanthropy.iupui.edu

Central Indiana Community Foundation: www.cicf.org

Charity Navigator: www.charitynavigator.org

Chicago Hope Academy: www.chicagohopeacademy.com

Council on Foundations: www.cof.org

The David and Lucile Packard Foundation: www.packard.org

Desert Reach: www.newbeginningschurch.com/reach.htm

Economic Opportunities (EcOp): www.mlfonline.org

Evangelical Council for Financial Accountability: www.ecfa.org

Family House: www.always.org.uk/familyhouse/

Faith and Service Technical Education Network (FASTEN): www.fastennetwork.org

Fellowship of Christian Athletes: www.fca.org

Friends of the Children: www.friendsofthechildren.org

The Gathering: www.gatheringweb.com

Generous Giving: www.generousgiving.org

Girl Scouts of the USA: www.girlscouts.org

Grantmakers for Effective Organizations: www.geofunders.org

Grantmakers Without Borders: www.internationaldonors.org

Greater Houston Community Foundation: www.ghcf.org

GuideStar: www.guidestar.org

Hope Christian Community Foundation: www.hopeccf.org

The Hudson Institute: www.hudson.org

Hugh O'Brian Youth Leadership Foundation: www.hoby.org

InnerChange Freedom Initiative: www.ifiprison.org

J. D. Levy & Associates, LLC: www.jdlevyassociates.com

Jewish Funders Network: www.jfunders.org

Kids Hope USA: www.kidshopeusa.org

Kingdom Oil: www.kingdomoil.org

The Legacy Group: www.philanthropyatwork.com

Maclellan Foundation: www.maclellanfoundation.org

The Manhattan Institute: www.manhattaninstitute.org

The Mary Reynolds Babcock Foundation: www.mrbf.org

Memphis Leadership Foundation: www.mlfonline.org

The Milton S. Eisenhower Foundation: www.eisenhowerfoundation.org

Ministry Watch: www.ministrywatch.com

My Friend's House: www.myfriendshouse.org

National Center for Neighborhood Enterprise: www.ncne.com

National Christian Foundation: www.nationalchristian.com

One by One Leadership: www.onebyoneleadership.com

Performance Results, Inc.: www.performance-results.net

Pew Forum on Religion and Public Life: www.pewforum.org

Philanthropy Roundtable: www.philanthropyroundtable.org

Prison Fellowship International: www.pfi.org

Pura Vida Coffee: www.puravidacoffee.org or www.puravidacoffee.com

The Roberts Enterprise Development Fund: www.redf.org

Rockwell Fund, Inc.: www.rockfund.org

Southeastern Council of Foundations: www.secf.org

Step 13: www.step13.org

Teen Challenge: www.teenchallenge.com

United Jewish Communities: www.ujc.org

United Way: http://national.unitedway.org/

Urban Ventures Leadership Foundation: www.urbanventures.org

Urban Youth Initiative: www.mlfonline.org

U.S. International Grantmaking Project of the Council on Foundations: www.usig.org

Victory Fellowship: www.victoryfellowship.com

Wilder Foundation: www.wilder.org

Young Life: www.younglife.org

Also available from Templeton Foundation Press

Street Saints
Renewing America's Cities

By Barbara J. Elliott

1-932031-76-6   Hardcover $24.95

TO ORDER: www.templetonpress.org   1-800-621-2736

Street Saints takes you through the streets of America's cities to meet people of faith who are renewing America, one heart at a time. It is a book of motivational stories about unsung heroes and a sociological study of the "faith factor," documenting faith-based programs that are treating social maladies in America. *Street Saints* profiles the motivated people responsible for these initiatives, the programs they are running, and the communities they are renewing. It offers inspiration, role models, and guidelines for people who would like to give back to their own communities.

From eight years of hands-on experience and more than three hundred interviews across the country, Barbara J. Elliott introduces us to the remarkable people who are street saints. She analyzes their best practices, their track records, what works, and why. She concludes by showing how these people and their inspirational services fit into the historical framework within which the United States has defined itself since its founding. Barbara Elliott shines a light on the spiritual reasons people engage in this kind of work and she provides a roadmap for people who are looking to make a difference.

"No one tells the stories of the nation's Good Samaritans with more warmth and intelligence than Barbara Elliott. Few grasp as clearly why faith commitment is crucial to family and social stability. In *Street Saints* we now have the most thorough treatment available of how religious groups of every stripe are revitalizing America's streets, neighborhoods and cities."

—*Joe Loconte, William E. Simon Fellow in Religion and a Free Society, at The Heritage Foundation*